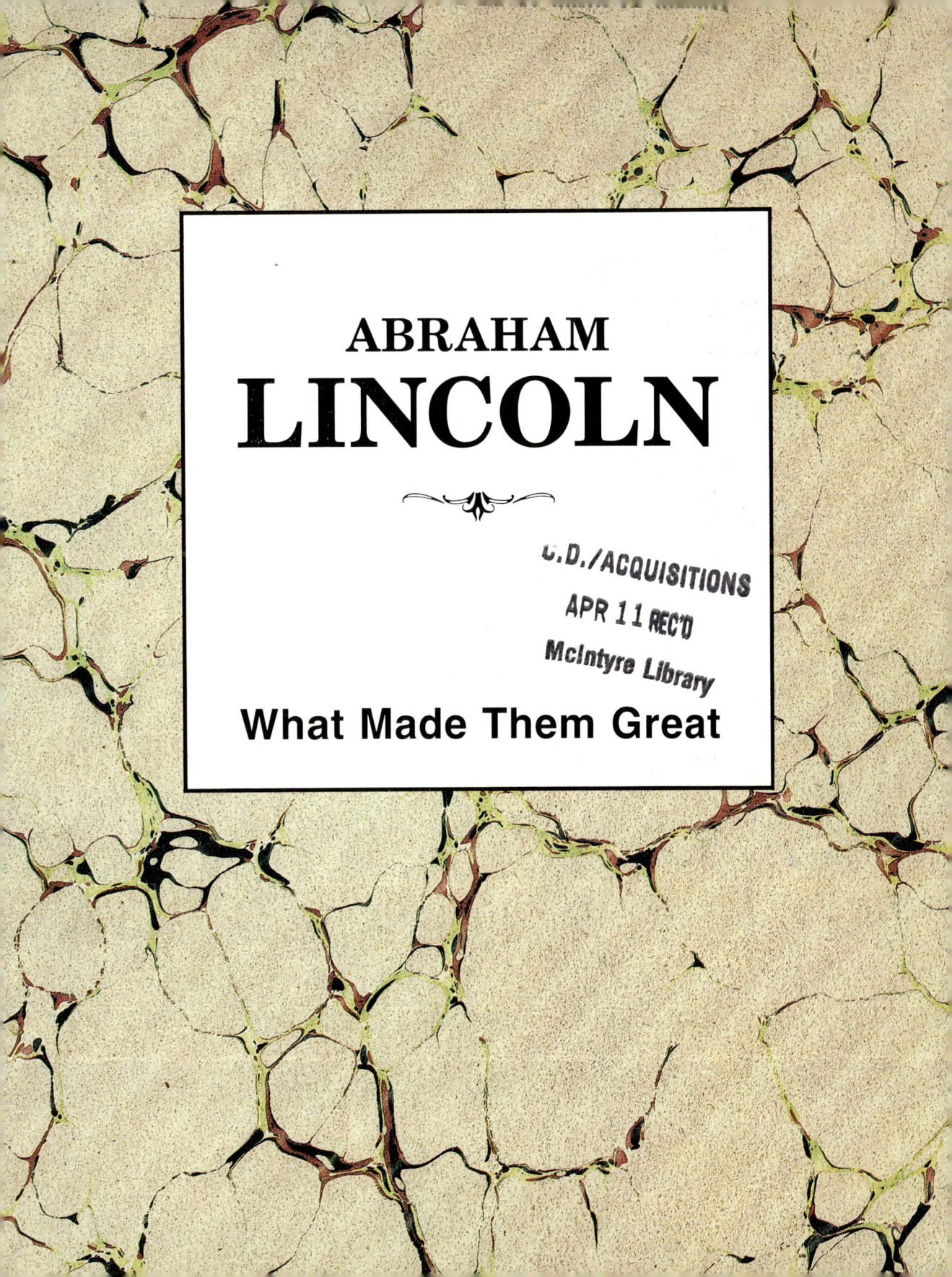

ABRAHAM LINCOLN

What Made Them Great

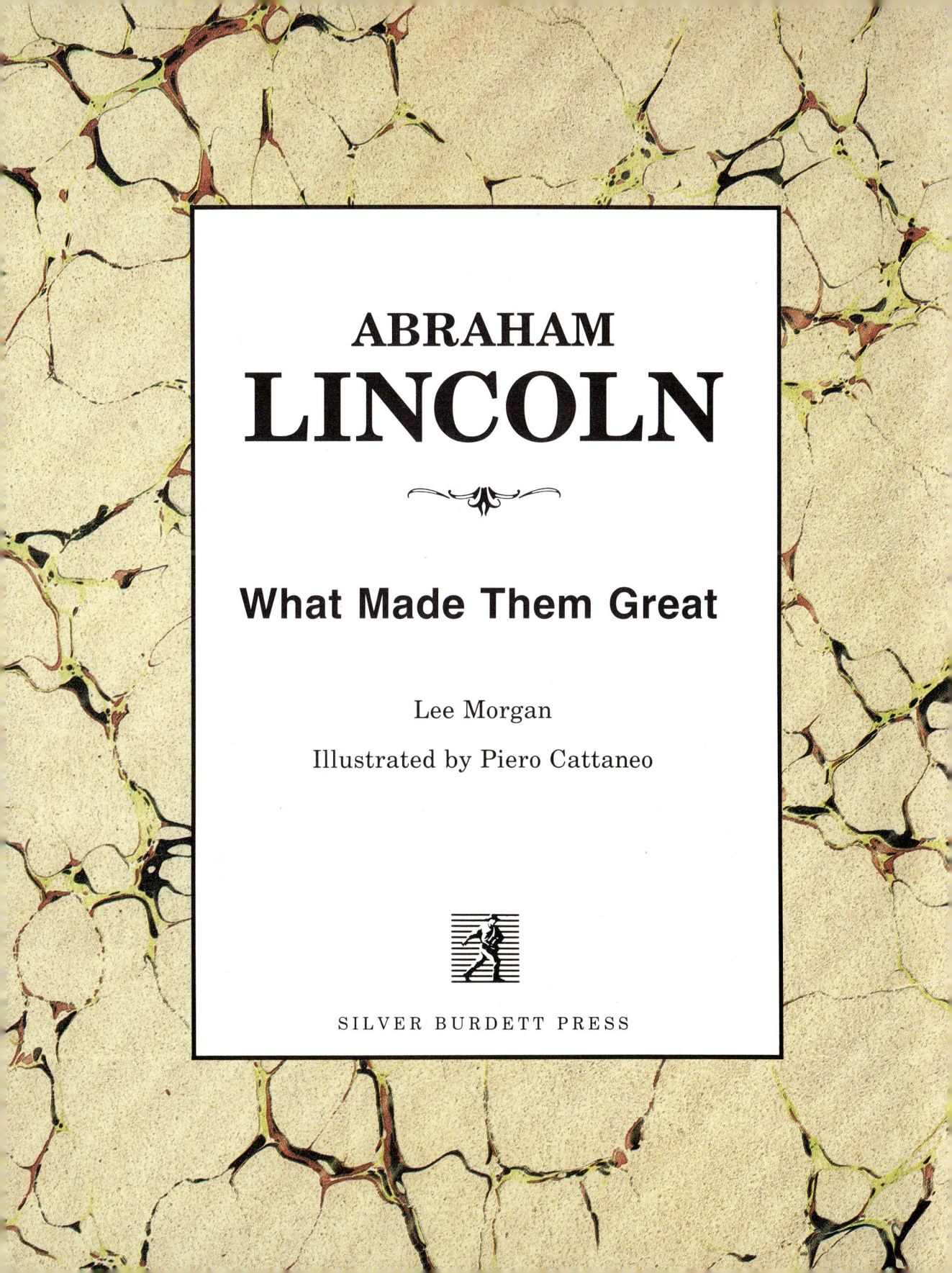

ABRAHAM LINCOLN

What Made Them Great

Lee Morgan

Illustrated by Piero Cattaneo

SILVER BURDETT PRESS

ACKNOWLEDGMENTS

We would like to thank David A. Williams, Professor Emeritus, Department of History, California State University, Long Beach; and Diane Sielski, Library Supervisor, Coldwater Exempted Village Schools, Ohio for their guidance and helpful suggestions.

Project Editor: Emily Easton (Silver Burdett Press)

Adapted and reformatted from the original by Kirchoff/Wohlberg, Inc.

Project Director: John R. Whitman
Graphics Coordinator: Jessica A. Kirchoff
Production Coordinator: Marianne Hile

Library of Congress Cataloging-in-Publication Data

Morgan, Lee, 1934—
    Abraham Lincoln/Lee Morgan; illustrated by Piero Cattaneo.
    p. cm.—[FROM SERIES: What Made Them Great]

Adaptation of: Abraham Lincoln/Lino Monchieri; translated by Mary Lee Grisanti.
    © 1985 Silver Burdett Company, Morristown, New Jersey.
    [FROM SERIES: Why They Became Famous]
    Includes bibliographical references.
Summary: Recounts the life of the dedicated man who survived a difficult childhood, became a country lawyer, and as sixteenth president of the United States, guided the country during the Civil War.
  1. Lincoln, Abraham, 1809-1865—Juvenile literature. 2. Presidents—United States—Biography—Juvenile literature. [1. Lincoln, Abraham, 1809-1865. 2. Presidents.]
    I. Cattaneo, Piero, ill. II. Monchieri, Lino. Perchè Sono Diventati Famosi. III. Series.

E457.905.M65 1990   973.7'092—dc20   [B]   [92]   89-38688   CIP   AC

Copyright © 1990 Silver Burdett Press. All rights reserved including the right of reproduction in whole or in part in any form. Published by Silver Burdett Press, a division of Simon & Schuster, Inc. Englewood Cliffs, New Jersey. Manufactured in Italy.

© Fabbri Editori S.p.A., Milan 1981
Translated into English by Mary Lee Grisanti for Silver Burdett Press from Perché Sono Diventati Famosi: Lincoln
First published in Italy in 1981 by Fabbri Editori S.p.A., Milan

10 9 8 7 6 5 4 3 2 1 (Library Binding)
10 9 8 7 6 5 4 3 2 1 (Softcover)

ISBN 0-382-09973-7 (Library Binding)
ISBN 0-382-24000-6 (Softcover)

TABLE OF CONTENTS

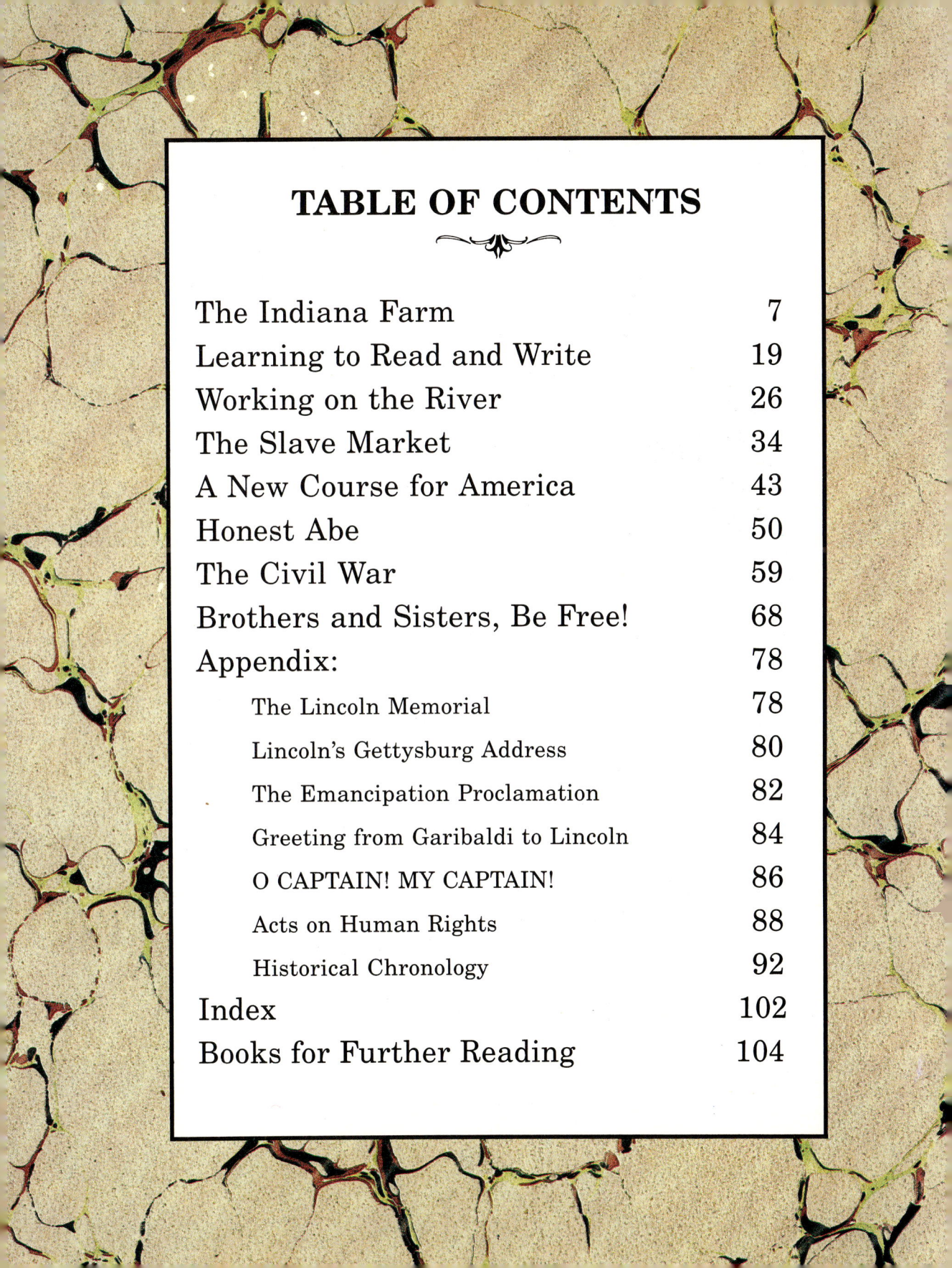

The Indiana Farm	7
Learning to Read and Write	19
Working on the River	26
The Slave Market	34
A New Course for America	43
Honest Abe	50
The Civil War	59
Brothers and Sisters, Be Free!	68
Appendix:	78
The Lincoln Memorial	78
Lincoln's Gettysburg Address	80
The Emancipation Proclamation	82
Greeting from Garibaldi to Lincoln	84
O CAPTAIN! MY CAPTAIN!	86
Acts on Human Rights	88
Historical Chronology	92
Index	102
Books for Further Reading	104

The Indiana Farm

On a freezing cold morning in December 1816, Thomas Lincoln, his wife Nancy, and their two children said good-bye to their log cabin. Like many Americans in those days, the Lincolns were moving west. They were leaving Kentucky and going to Indiana.

Tom Lincoln was a skilled carpenter. But this work no longer satisfied him. Instead, he dreamed of becoming a farmer and supporting his family by working the land. Several times he had bought farms in Kentucky and then sold them. Tom was a restless sort of man. He was always looking for a special place. Exactly where this spot was he could not say.

He wanted a place where he would not have to depend on anyone except himself.

Some time earlier, Tom had been tracking wild boar in Indiana. He had noticed a promising plot of land. Perhaps this might finally be the special place he had been seeking. He decided to move his family there. Now they were on their way to their home. It would be on the Ohio River in Indiana.

Tom and Nancy were used to hardships. Their two children, Abraham and Sarah, had been born in a crude log cabin. When the family decided to leave Kentucky, they hoped this move would be the last. With no regrets, they packed their few belongings into a wagon. Then they set out down the road toward a new life.

Wintry winds roared through the leafless forests. The trails leading west were rough and winding. After four days they reached the Ohio River. There they crossed the river on a ferryboat. When the ferryman set them down on the opposite bank, they were in Indiana. Tom had the expert eye of a hunter. He had no trouble locating his land.

"All this is ours," he said proudly to his family. "It's been measured and registered with the Land Office."

At first, Nancy could not help feeling a little disappointed. "But this is just a forest," she told her husband. "There are no other families or farms for miles around."

Tom tried to make her feel better. He reminded her that it was always hard at first. But next spring they could begin clearing the trees. From the logs they would build a beautiful new house.

But Nancy still worried. What would they eat during the winter? How could they fill their stomachs until summer and the first harvest?

"The forest," replied Tom. "Until our crops are ready, the forest is ours. There's plenty of wild game and nuts and fruits."

Young Abe Lincoln was seven when his family arrived in Indiana. Already he was able to help with many of the chores. Like his father, he deeply loved the land and all the plants and animals living on it. He also had Tom Lincoln's ability to work hard. He was proud of what he could do.

That winter, storms pounded Indiana. The air was icy with sleet and snow. The Lincoln family lived in a lean-to with only three sides. The shack barely protected them from the cold. Day and night they had to keep a fire burning. The nearest water was a mile away. Living was hard.

In the spring they began cutting down trees. Now they could build a real cabin. Tom was an expert woodsman, and Abe took after his father. Soon the boy was able to handle an axe with ease and skill.

The only thing Abe could not manage to do was hunt. He understood that you had to kill an animal to eat. Finding and tracking game was easy. But no

matter how hard he tried, something always stopped him from shooting.

Only once did Abe manage to actually pull the trigger. He killed a wild turkey. The bird fell to the ground and bled slowly to death. Watching in horror, he turned to his father.

"Pa, can one shot like that kill a man?"

His father nodded.

"Have you ever killed a man?"

"No, Son."

"Well, have you ever seen a man get shot?"

Tom Lincoln's face grew sad. "I have," he said quietly. "I saw my own father die from a gunshot wound. His name was Abraham. Just like yours."

Abe was curious. "How did such a terrible thing happen?"

But his father looked away. "Someday I'll tell you all about it. Listen here, your mother will need time to get that turkey cooked for supper. Let's go home now."

Returning to the cabin, they stopped for a moment to admire their handiwork. The entire family had helped build the house. Tom and Abe had chopped down trees to make the logs. Nancy and Sarah had peeled away the bark to make the logs smooth. Together, they all dragged the logs from the woods to the spot where the cabin would stand.

Every inch of the cabin had been built with their own hands.

The floor was made of beaten clay. A handsome stone fireplace heated the whole cabin. Every table, every chair, every chest of drawers was made from the wood of their own trees. At night, they slept on mattresses stuffed with dry leaves.

As Tom and Abe gazed around, they could not help feeling pleased and proud.

"What a wonderful house!" exclaimed Tom.

"It's nothing like that shivery old lean-to where we spent the winter," Abe said.

His father agreed. The house was sturdy. It was built to last for many years.

"What'll happen to the lean-to now?" Abe wondered.

"Well, your mother's kin will be coming from Kentucky soon. All your Sparrow relatives and your cousin Dennis Hanks will be here. That shack will be fine for them to use for a while."

Abe was thrilled to learn that company was coming. He jumped up and down in excitement.

Tom's eyes twinkled. That was exactly how Nancy Lincoln felt about it. Both he and Abe knew how much she missed the company of other women.

"But Pa," Abe said. "Won't the Sparrows want a better house than the lean-to?"

"Sure they will. And when the time comes, we'll help them build a fine place just like ours."

His father added, "And maybe your cousin Dennis can teach you a few things about hunting."

Abe made a face. "Ugh. I don't want to kill anything. I just hate it, Pa."

Throwing his arm around Abe's shoulder, Tom began to tease. He hadn't noticed his son hating meat when it got to his plate.

Together they went into the cabin.

That evening, Abe could not forget what he had heard about his grandfather. His father had promised to finish the story. Fidgeting, Abe waited for the right moment to bring up the subject.

After supper, Tom sat near the fire smoking his pipe.

"Pa," Abe called out, "we're ready now."

"Ready for bed?" his father laughed.

"Ready for the story you promised."

Tom Lincoln blew a smoke ring in the air and heaved a sigh. Someday he had planned to tell this painful story to his children. He supposed it might as well be now.

Still, it was hard to begin. "We were living in Kentucky then," he said. "One day my father and my brothers, Joshua and Mordecai, were working in the fields. I tagged along behind because I was too little to help. But I watched everything they did so I could learn."

"Learn what, Pa?" Sarah broke in.

Tom shrugged. "Oh, how to handle the horses—how to guide them. The furrows have to be straight, you know."

On that day, Tom continued, his father was doing the plowing. Suddenly a shot rang out; the noise sounded as loud as thunder. Tom's father clutched at his head. Then he fell to the ground.

As Tom went on speaking, Abe and Sarah grew silent. Their eyes were riveted on their father.

Tom's brothers ran into the house and left him alone there. He called his father's name. The blood poured from the wound and soaked the freshly plowed earth. Tom was frightened.

Then Tom looked up. Above him stood a huge Indian with a painted face. He wore a crown of feathers on his head. He was staring at Tom.

Even now Tom could still remember the Indian's eyes. "They glowed like fire. His lips began moving. He was just about to speak."

At that moment another shot was heard. Tom watched the Indian stiffen and drop to the ground like a bird shot in midair.

"Pa," Sarah cried, "what happened?"

"Mordecai shot him," Tom said. "From the window of our house."

"Weren't you scared?" Sarah asked.

Their father nodded. "I'll never forget that day. Right before my eyes people were dying. Not one, but two." In a quiet voice he added, "And death only missed me by a hair's breath."

Abe and his sister did not move. Then Abe asked, "Why did that Indian want to kill Grandpa?"

15

"Don't know," his father said. "Maybe hatred for men who had taken Indian land. Maybe revenge over a dead friend. Can't say."

The death of his father left Mordecai Lincoln with terrible scars. After that he hated all Indians. Whenever he saw an Indian, he wanted to shoot him. He never got over his anger either.

Abe bowed his head. In bed that night he lay awake thinking about the story.

The next year Tom and Betsy Sparrow arrived. Nancy Lincoln felt overjoyed to see the couple who had raised her. With them came Dennis Hanks, their nineteen-year-old nephew. The Sparrows hoped to build a home. They, too, would farm the rich Indiana land.

Not long afterward, a deadly disease, called milk sickness, spread through Indiana. The Sparrows become ill. Aches and pains were quickly followed by throbbing fever. Arms and legs turned icy cold. Tongues swelled. They were thirsty all the time.

In Indiana, there were no doctors or medical supplies. Like other victims of the disease, the Sparrows died. Their nephew Dennis moved in with the Lincolns.

Shortly after this tragedy, a woman on a nearby farm also fell ill. Nancy Lincoln insisted on nursing her neighbor.

A few days later Nancy began to show symptoms of the dreaded milk sickness. For a week,

she suffered horribly. During his wife's illness, Tom would not permit the children near her bedside. He feared they, too, would become infected. But as she lay dying, he allowed them to say good-bye.

Abe and Sarah hugged and kissed their mother for the last time. The next day Nancy Lincoln was buried in the forest. She was buried alongside the fresh graves of Tom and Betsy Sparrow.

Abe was quickly learning about the hardships of frontier life. Life often took cruel and unexpected turns. Sometimes people died at an early age. But hard work and the loss of his mother taught him lessons that he remembered all his life.

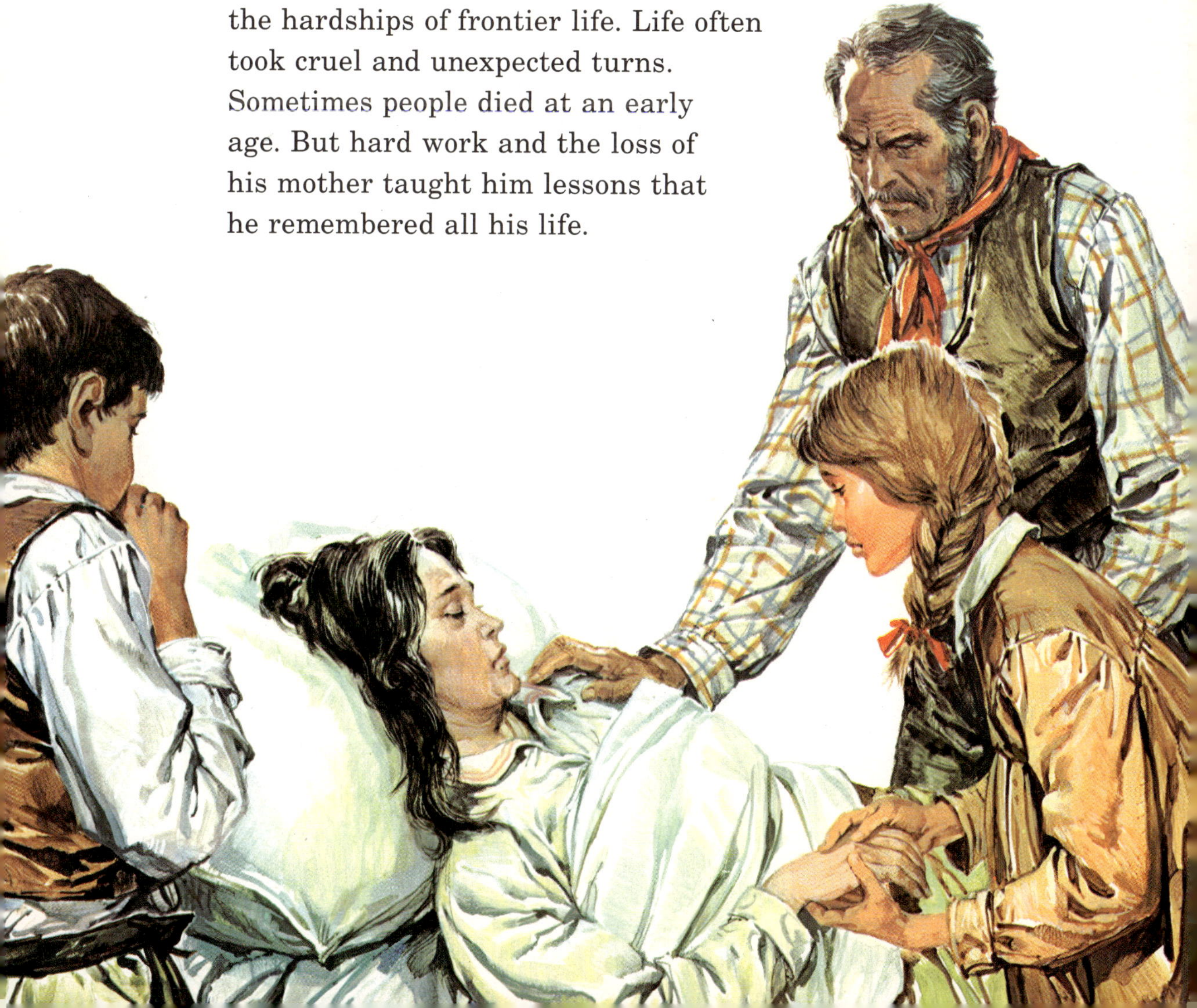

Learning to Read and Write

ife on the farm was hard and lonely. Twelve-year-old Sarah had to take over her mother's chores. Now it was her job to cook the food and mend the clothes. She did her best to keep the house clean.

Abe helped his father and Dennis Hanks. The horses, cows, and pigs had to be cared for. There were fields to plow and seeds to sow. Later the crops had to be harvested.

Sometimes there were disappointments. Once they had just finished plowing and planting. A bad storm blew up. A flood washed the seeds away. Everything had to be done over again.

In the woods around the cabin lurked wild animals. This country was still part of the western frontier. Sometimes the family's sleep was broken by the screams of panthers. Bears crept close to the farm and tried to kill the pigs. These animals scared Abe. When he was grown up, Abe wrote a poem about the dangers the Lincolns had to face.

The Lincoln family never had enough money. Many years later, people would ask Abe about his childhood. He always answered that his youth could be described in one short sentence: He was poor.

But their lives changed for the better in 1819. Thomas Lincoln married again. His new wife was Sarah Bush Johnston. She was a cheerful widow with three children of her own. Her daughters were named Elizabeth and Matilda. She also had a son named John.

Luckily, Sarah Lincoln had a little money of her own. She used it to make life easier for the Lincoln family. She wasted no time furnishing the cabin with comfortable furniture. Now curtains hung on the windows. For the first time, Abe's sister, Sarah, had a pretty dress to wear. The house rang with the sound of laughter.

Sarah wanted to be more than a stepmother to Tom's children. Instead, she tried to treat them like her own children.

Sarah Lincoln took a great liking to her stepson. Immediately, she noticed that Abe was an unusual boy. Indeed, she was the first to see that he was special.

"Abe's so bright," she said to Tom. "And he has so much character. I believe he'll be a great man when he grows up."

Tom hoped she was right. He would be glad if Abe did not become a farmer. No matter how hard Tom worked, he never made enough money. As a result, he was an unhappy man. He hoped his children would have happier and easier lives than he had had.

Abraham Lincoln never forgot the kindness of his stepmother. When he grew older, he called her "my angel mother." By then she knew that her opinion of Abe had been right. She lived to see him elected President.

Abe's stepmother loved to read. She owned many books. One of them was the Bible. Many nights he lay on the floor in front of the fire. By the light of the flames or by flickering candles he read the Scriptures. He also enjoyed adventure stories. Some of the adventures he liked were *Robinson Crusoe* and *The Arabian Nights*.

Reading became a habit for Abe. This pleased his stepmother. "That's the way to make something of yourself," she told him.

By and by, Abe's stepmother decided that he should attend school. It was important to learn reading, writing, and arithmetic.

Frontier schools were known as "blab" schools. Pupils were supposed to study out loud. As they leaned over their copy books, they had to speak whatever they were thinking. If anyone stopped talking, the teacher noticed immediately. It was thought that the student must be wasting time. To warn students to pay attention, the teacher hit them across the shoulders with a stick.

Abe was never beaten by the teacher's stick. He was eager to learn. And he was smart. Usually he finished his lessons ahead of everyone else.

One day the teacher asked, "What do we do with wood?"

Abe was the first to answer. "Why, we make things with wood," he said quickly. "Fences and cabins and boats. We also carve things. Like bookends and curtain rods."

"That's right, Abe," said the teacher. "You're good with words. Maybe you'll become a writer someday."

Like most pioneer children, Abe's time in school did not last long. He was needed to work on the farm. He attended school for only about one year.

But in that one year he learned something important. He learned how to read well and write carefully. Now he knew how to study. He set about learning on his own. He borrowed books. Sometimes he walked miles to find a copy of *Pilgrim's Progress* or *Aesop's Fables*. He read a life of George Washington. As he worked around the farm, he always carried a book with him.

Abe was growing up. Now he was tall and skinny. He had a good sense of humor. He was good at telling stories and jokes. Everybody liked the friendly young man. Sometimes farmers asked him to help them out with their chores.

But farm work bored him. One of his favorite jobs was working on the ferry that took passengers across the Ohio River between Indiana and Kentucky. Soon he knew plenty about the river—its swirling currents, its shallows, its rocks. He built a boat of his own.

One day two men came running down to the riverbank just as a steamboat was leaving. But they were too late. Spotting Abe with his rowboat, the men wondered if he could catch the steamboat.

"Jump in," Abe cried. "I'll put you aboard."

He began rowing as hard as he could. They reached the steamboat just in time.

Abe's passengers climbed up to the deck. Each of the men tossed Abe a silver half dollar. He could hardly believe that he had earned a dollar so easily.

Working on the River

Up and down the big river paraded the steamboats with their tall smokestacks. Some were traveling upstream to Cincinnati. Others were going south to the city of New Orleans. For two years Abe worked as a ferryman. He took passengers out to the middle of the river. There they boarded the big steamboats.

The richest man in town was James Gentry. He owned a general store. Gentry wanted to send his son Allen to New Orleans to sell corn and hogs. In

those years, the best way to ship farm products was by boat. But Allen had no skill with boats. Gentry asked for Abe's help, and he eagerly agreed. At nineteen, Abe was glad for the chance to travel and see a bit of the world.

He and Allen built a flatboat made of logs. Soon their great adventure was under way. The trip was 1,200 miles. During the day they guided the raft downstream. At night, they tied up along the riverbank and slept.

In New Orleans, they sold Mr. Gentry's corn and pork. With the money, they bought clothing and tools for the Gentry store. Then they walked around,

taking in the sights. New Orleans was one of the biggest cities in the country. Abe was absolutely amazed. Along the waterfront he saw hundreds of ships. Bales of cotton crowded the wharves. There was the clink of coins as cotton and tobacco were sold.

In the wealthy sections of New Orleans people wore fine clothing. They lived in great mansions. The sight made Abe stop and stare.

"Just think," he said to Allen. "A lot of poor people must work for those rich families." Why did a few people have so much in life? And why did other folks have so little? He felt sorry for the poor.

Back home in Indiana, James Gentry paid him twenty-four dollars. The New Orleans trip was Abe's first taste of success.

Abe went back to working as a ferryman. He took people out to the steamboats. And he also carried travelers across the river to Kentucky. Or he picked them up there and returned to Indiana.

It happened that crossing the river caused Abe to break the law accidentally. In Indiana, a ferryman did not need a license. But unknown to Abe, Kentucky law was different. In that state a license was necessary. So every time Abe left passengers on the Kentucky shore he was breaking the law.

A jealous ferryman reported Abe to the police. As a result, Abe had to appear before a judge. The crime was not serious. Abe got off, promising never to take passengers to Kentucky again.

For the first time Abe saw a court of law. Fascinated, he wanted to learn more about the legal system. How was a person's guilt or innocence really decided? He decided to study law. Every chance he got, he attended court. He liked listening to cases being argued.

When Abe was twenty-one, the Lincoln family moved again. For a long while now, Tom Lincoln felt he had failed at farming in Indiana. Perhaps he could do better some place else. Abe's cousin John Hanks had sent them glowing reports about the state of Illinois.

Abe was in favor of moving. "There's plenty of land in Illinois," he said. "Let's go."

So in 1830 the Lincolns set out for Illinois, some two hundred miles west. Their belongings were piled on three wagons.

The trip was slow. It was difficult to cover even a few miles each day. The way took them through heavy forests. There were no good roads. Whenever they came to a stream, Abe and Dennis searched for a shallow place to cross. Not until they found a ford could the wagons keep moving.

At last they reached the flat prairie of Illinois. It was in this state that Abe would someday make a name for himself. At the town of Decatur, near the Sangamon River, the Lincolns met John Hanks.

After their arrival, Abe helped his father clear the land and plant their first crop. There were rails

to be split and another log cabin to be built. The Lincoln women did their best to make their new home comfortable.

In Illinois Abe saw an opportunity to make money. Other farmers had also recently settled along the Sangamon River. All of them needed fences around their property. This was the only way to show where one farm ended and the next one began. And the fences kept livestock from wandering away.

In those days fences were made of posts planted in the ground. In between the posts ran long rails. This meant chopping down trees and cutting off the branches. Then the trunks had to be split lengthwise. The job was backbreaking. It also took time, and farmers were busy. They liked to hire someone to split their rails.

Abe hired out as a rail-splitter. It is said that he split over two thousand rails. That's how he got to be known as "Abe Lincoln, the Rail-Splitter."

Before long Abe had made many friends. One of them was a storekeeper named Denton Offutt. Offutt wanted to trade goods down the Mississippi. After hearing about Abe's trip to New Orleans, Offutt had an idea.

"How about making a trip with my cargo?" he asked Abe.

Abe thought about it. On this trip he could take along his cousin John Hanks and his stepbrother John Johnston.

"Sounds fine," he said. "Where's your boat?"

"Boat?" Offutt looked surprised. "Why, I haven't got a boat. Never thought of that!"

Abe laughed. "Don't worry, Mr. Offutt. We'll build you a boat."

In one month they had a flatboat completed. Oblong shaped, it was large enough to carry barrels of corn, crates of coon skins, and cages full of hogs. Two long oars, one at each end, steered the boat.

The big moment finally arrived. Abe, John Hanks, and John Johnston proudly went aboard. With them was Offutt, who wanted to ride along on the first leg of the journey.

They had not traveled very far when disaster struck. They came to a dam and tried to float over it. But the water was too shallow. They got stuck on top of the dam. Water began to soak the cargo.

"What'll we do?" shouted John Hanks.

Abe had to think of a plan quickly. "First we'd better lighten the boat," he said.

The men scrambled to unload part of the cargo. They bored a hole in the bottom to let the water drain out. After sliding the boat over the dam, they plugged the hole again. Finally, they reloaded the cargo and continued on their way.

Denton Offutt felt greatly relieved. He decided Abe was good at solving problems. The businessman stepped off the boat and waved good-bye. As the cargo drifted out of sight, he knew it was in good hands.

The Slave Market

They reached New Orleans, with no further problems. Abe sold Denton Offutt's cargo. Then he sold his boat and arranged to return home on one of the steamboats heading north up the Mississippi.

While waiting for the riverboat, Abe showed his stepbrother around. Exploring the city, they came across a strange sight. It was a tall wooden platform.

Nearby were huddled three men and two women. They were tied together by chains.

Abe and John saw signs that read "Slaves for Sale." Some of the signs advertised men as "suitable for hardest work." Others described women who were "experienced at picking cotton."

Abe said angrily, "Those people there will be sold to the highest bidder. They're chained up so they can't escape."

"But that's the way cattle are sold," John said.

"That's right," Abe said. "Slave owners sell people like they're animals. If I ever get a chance to hit this sort of thing, I'll hit it hard."

By accident, Abe and his stepbrother had stumbled into the New Orleans slave market. In the South, the big cotton and sugarcane plantations constantly needed workers. The work was brutal and hard. Many slaves died. That was why plantation owners always had to buy more slaves.

Slaves lived in dread of being shipped to New Orleans. They called it being "sold down the river." Today that term is still used when people talk about being betrayed.

In the days when Abe Lincoln visited New Orleans many Americans were having furious arguments about slavery. Indeed, there was no subject that made people angrier. New states were being added to the Union all the time. Some of these states insisted on the right to own slaves. This idea was opposed by people who wanted to keep slave states from joining the Union. In that way, they hoped that the spread of slavery could be stopped.

As Abe and his stepbrother watched, the slave sale began. A man climbed up on the platform. He ordered the slaves unchained. One by one they were brought up to be shown.

"Great bargains!" the auctioneer shouted. "All hale and hearty. Come on now. What'm I bid?"

Buyers yelled out their bids. In no time at all, the three men and two women had been sold. Their new owners hustled them away.

Next a little girl was pushed onto the platform. The auctioneer called for bids. Below the platform, a woman began screaming. She tried to rush forward and save the little girl. A man with a whip forced her back. The child was sold and taken away. Her mother began to sob. She knew she would never see her daughter again.

Abe and John stared in horror. They had never seen slaves before. It was hard to imagine anyone in the backwoods of Illinois owning slaves. The farmers had a hard time feeding themselves. How could they also afford to feed slaves?

But Abe doubted that even rich people up North wanted slaves. There were no plantations needing workers. In the North businesses paid their labor. Of course workers at home toiled very hard, too. But at least they were free, he thought.

Slavery was wrong. Watching the sale of the girl made him understand how awful it really was.

John said to him, "Something ought to be done about this."

Abe turned to his stepbrother. "Something will be done. But I don't know what."

They had seen as much as they could stand. Slowly they walked away.

At the dock, their steamboat was ready to go. Soon they were on their way home to New Salem. But they could not forget what they had just seen.

"You know," John said, "they say that cotton is king in the South."

Abe recalled hearing the same words. The South grew cotton and sold it to other countries. Much of their cotton went to England. The English always needed cotton because they spun it into cloth. English cloth was sold all over the world. In the American South, slaves picked cotton. If they didn't pick enough they were beaten. King Cotton seemed to rule the lives of both slave and slaveowner.

Their trip home was slow and lazy. The rhythms of the river filled their ears. The water washed by. Soon their adventure would be over.

"What will you do back home?" John asked.

"Mr. Offutt offered me a job in his store," Abe said. "Maybe I'll take it."

John grinned at him. "You should go into politics," he said.

"Well, maybe I will someday. But first I'd have to get people to back me up."

"Ask Andy Jackson to help you," he teased.

"Sure," Abe laughed. "Andy Jackson will never hear of me. I'm only a poor farmer."

Andy Jackson was Andrew Jackson, the president of the United States. Under Jackson, the economy of the country was prospering. Everywhere change was in the air. More factories opened. Bankers created new wealth. The great cities like New York and Boston would soon double in size.

With Jackson in the White House, most people had little to complain about. They were living well. Few Americans stopped to wonder about how the slaves were doing. They knew nothing about life as a slave. The true story of slavery had never been told.

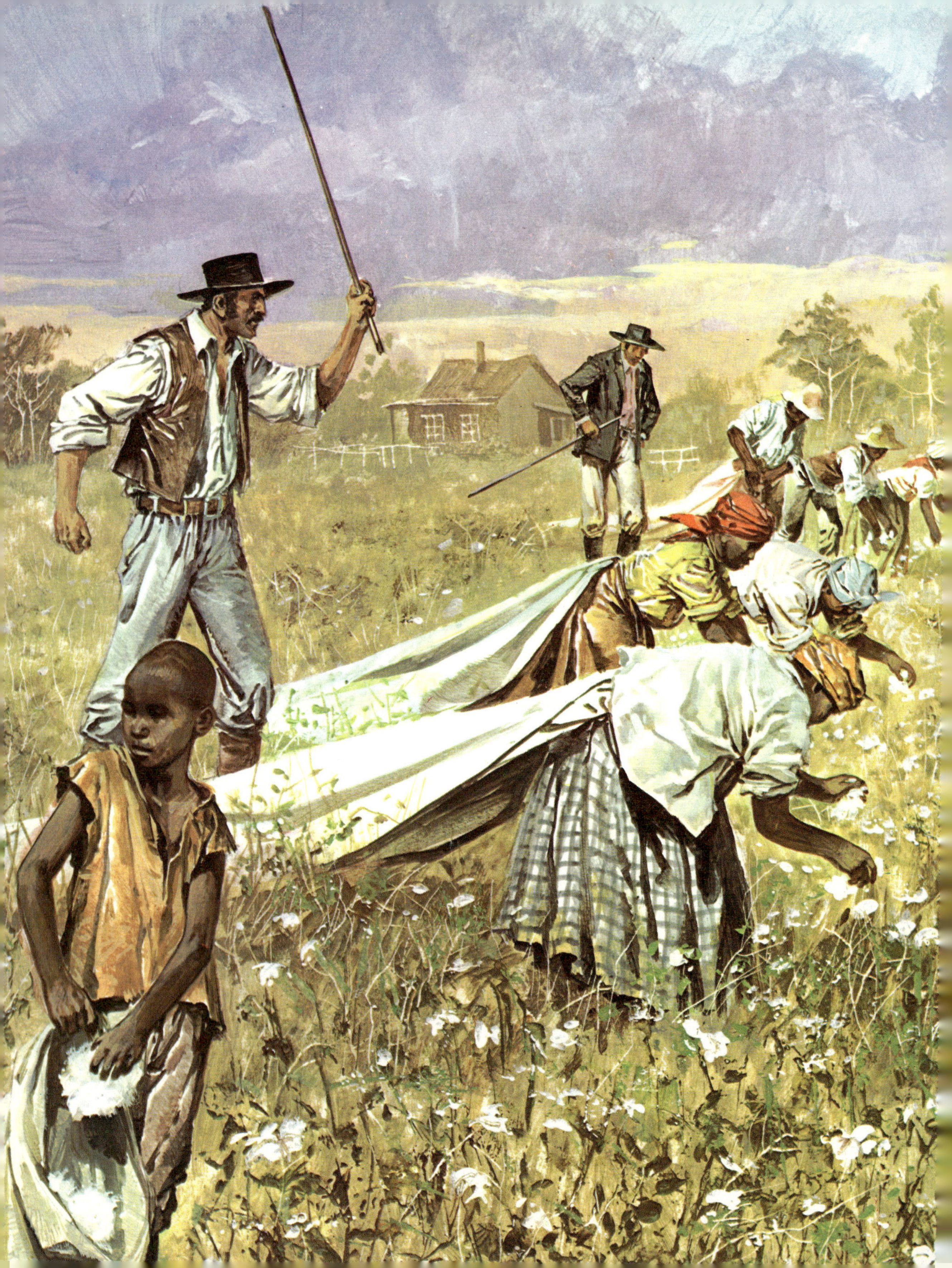

It would be yet another twenty years before Harriet Beecher Stowe published *Uncle Tom's Cabin*. This was the first popular novel to describe the lives of slaves. The hero is Uncle Tom, a black man who never loses his dignity. The villain, Simon Legree, is a cruel boss.

In *Uncle Tom's Cabin*, slaveowners are shown living in luxury. All the hard work is done by blacks. They live in poor cabins. They sleep on piles of straw and eat poor food. A lucky few work inside their masters' houses. But the rest go out into the fields and work under the broiling sun. From dawn to dusk they pick cotton.

Harriet Beecher Stowe's novel was read all over America. Many Southerners felt angry. They disliked the harsh way in which she pictured slavery. Northerners generally admired the book. They believed it told the truth. So people continued to hold different opinions about slavery.

Uncle Tom's Cabin helped to bring about the Civil War. The book convinced Northerners that slavery was an evil system. No matter what, it had to be stopped.

Years later, Harriet Beecher Stowe visited the White House. It was during the war, and Abe was president. When he met the writer, he smiled and called her "the little lady who started the big war."

However, all this lay far in the future as young Abe steamed home to New Salem.

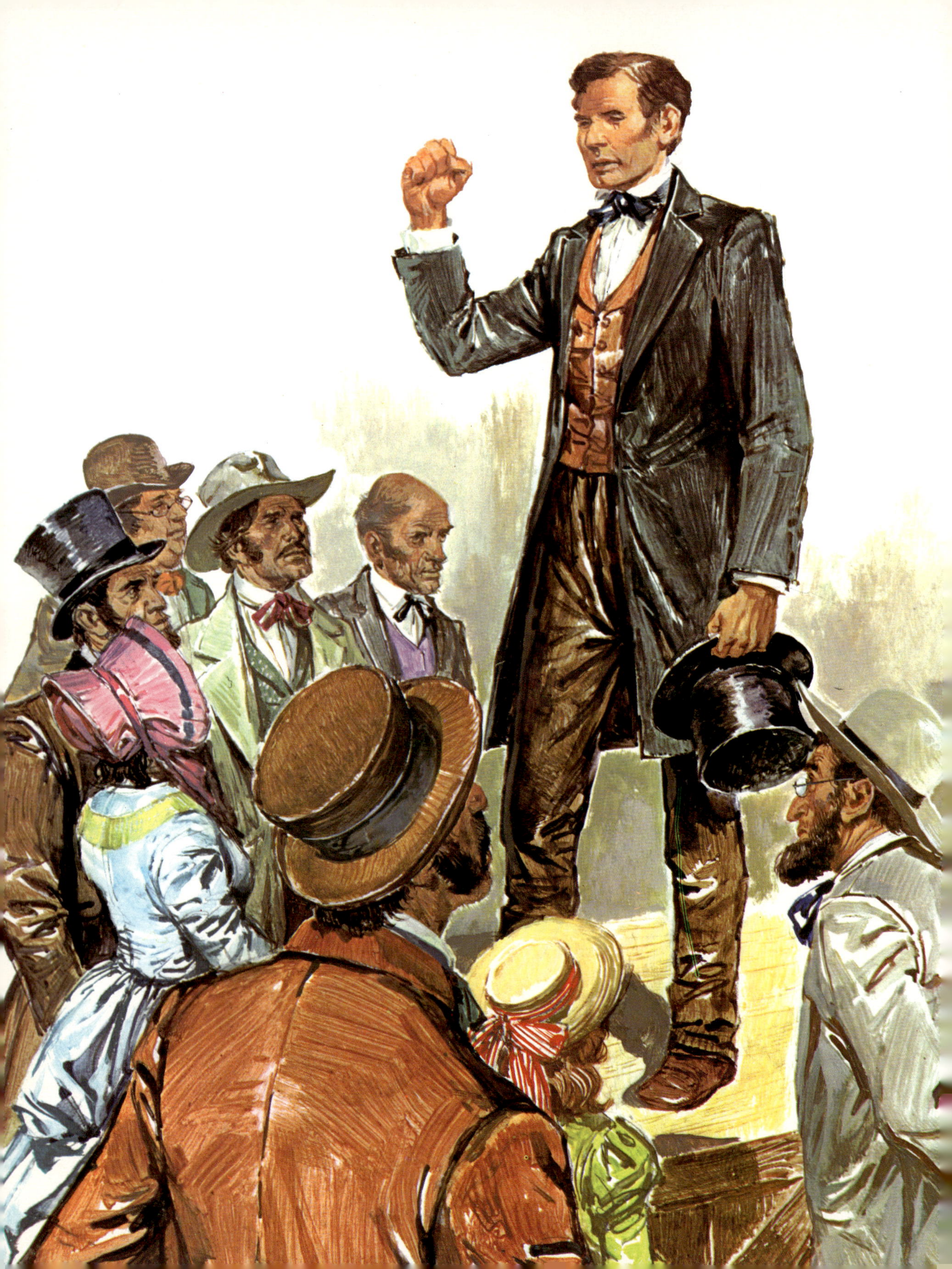

A New Course for America

In New Salem, Abe worked as a clerk in Denton Offutt's store. He sold groceries and clothing. His wages as a clerk were fifteen dollars a month.

New Salem was a tiny frontier town. At that time a gang of rough young men lived there. Their leader was a man named Jack Armstrong. Abe's popularity made him jealous.

One day, Armstrong challenged Abe to a wrestling match. "We'll see who's the strongest," he bragged. He believed that he was.

Abe didn't like fighting, but he accepted Armstrong's challenge.

A large crowd showed up to watch. The fight did not last long. Abe knocked Jack down and pinned him to the ground. Afterwards, Jack became one of Abe's best friends.

In 1832, the Black Hawk War was being fought in western Illinois. Indians and settlers battled. Abe and Jack volunteered. The company marched off, but the only Indian they saw was one peaceful old man. Abe saved him from being killed.

After the Black Hawk War, Abe's interest in politics began to grow. Maybe it could be his career.

He ran for a seat in the state legislature, which made laws for the people in Illinois. Campaigning hard, he made speeches all over his district. But he lost the election.

Abe and a friend decided to buy a store together. Unfortunately, the store failed. Then his partner died. There were many debts. Abe promised to repay everyone. Because he did, the people in New Salem began calling him "Honest Abe."

In 1833 he was appointed postmaster. It was his job to deliver all the mail arriving in New Salem. As postmaster he got to know the voters. When he ran for the state legislature again, he won.

Meanwhile Abe had decided to become a lawyer. Borrowing books, he began studying law. In his spare time he read Supreme Court decisions.

Once a friend noticed him lying on a woodpile. Abe had a book in his hand. "What's that you're reading?" the friend asked.

"Oh, I'm not just reading," Abe said. "I'm studying law."

Now Abe spent most of his time in Vandalia, the capital of Illinois. He became a member of the Whig Party. The Whigs opposed the Democrats and President Andrew Jackson. Abe personally believed that Jackson didn't do enough to help the states.

In the Illinois House of Representatives, Abe stood up and talked about how badly their state needed roads and bridges. But they could not depend on Jackson to provide these things. "We have to do the job ourselves," he declared.

By this time Abe was twenty-six years old. Most men his age had wives and children. A story is told about why Abe was still not married. The story says that he fell in love with the daughter of a local tavernkeeper. Her name was Ann Rutledge.

But tragedy supposedly prevented their marriage. Ann died suddenly. It is said that her death left Abe shattered.

There is no basis to this romantic lover's tale. In later years Abe never mentioned a love affair with Ann. Most likely the legend started after he became president. No scholars today believe it. But the story of Abe and Ann continues to be told.

In his middle twenties, Abe was not worried about finding a wife. He was busy teaching himself the law. Once he had learned enough on his own, he was able to pass the bar examination. After 1836, he began taking clients and defending them in court.

Soon he became known for his ability to judge evidence. For example, he was always quick to spot the strong points in a client's defense. Rival lawyers soon learned that. Abe also was quick to notice the weak parts of their arguments.

The people he helped were often farmers. Many of his cases were argued in county courts. That meant he rode for miles through the countryside. He was known as a "prairie lawyer."

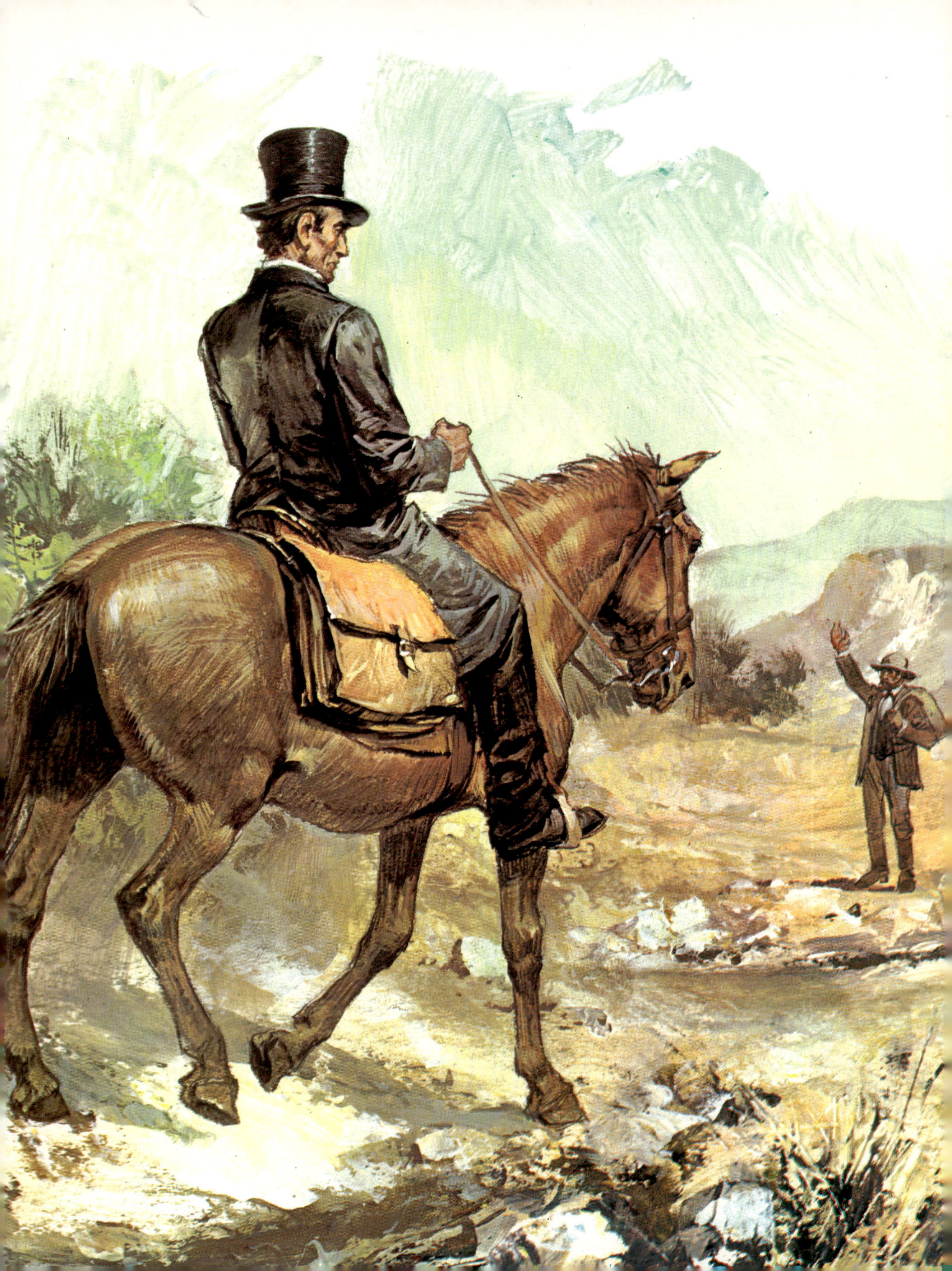

On these rides he had a chance to talk with many people. He learned how they felt about government in Illinois. And he heard what they thought about the national government in Washington. Slowly Abe began to form his own opinions about how the country should be run.

"Ought to be a bridge over that river," a farmer once complained to Abe. "Hard to get corn to market when you have to travel miles to a ford."

"Maybe I can get you a bridge," Abe said. "Wait until the state legislature meets. I sure will try my best."

After the next session of the legislature, the farmers got their bridge. Around New Salem, people said that Abe kept his promises. He wasn't called "Honest Abe" for nothing.

In 1837 the capital of Illinois moved from Vandalia to Springfield. It was in Springfield that Abe happened to meet a young woman visiting from Kentucky. Her name was Mary Todd.

Meeting at a dance, Abe and Mary liked each other at once. Mary Todd came from a wealthy and cultured family. She played the piano and spoke French. Some people said she was difficult to get along with. They said she was spoiled and had a bad temper. But Abe admired her lively spirit.

Mary certainly seemed to be the opposite of Abe Lincoln, who was shy and had plain country manners. Nobody was surprised when Abe fell in

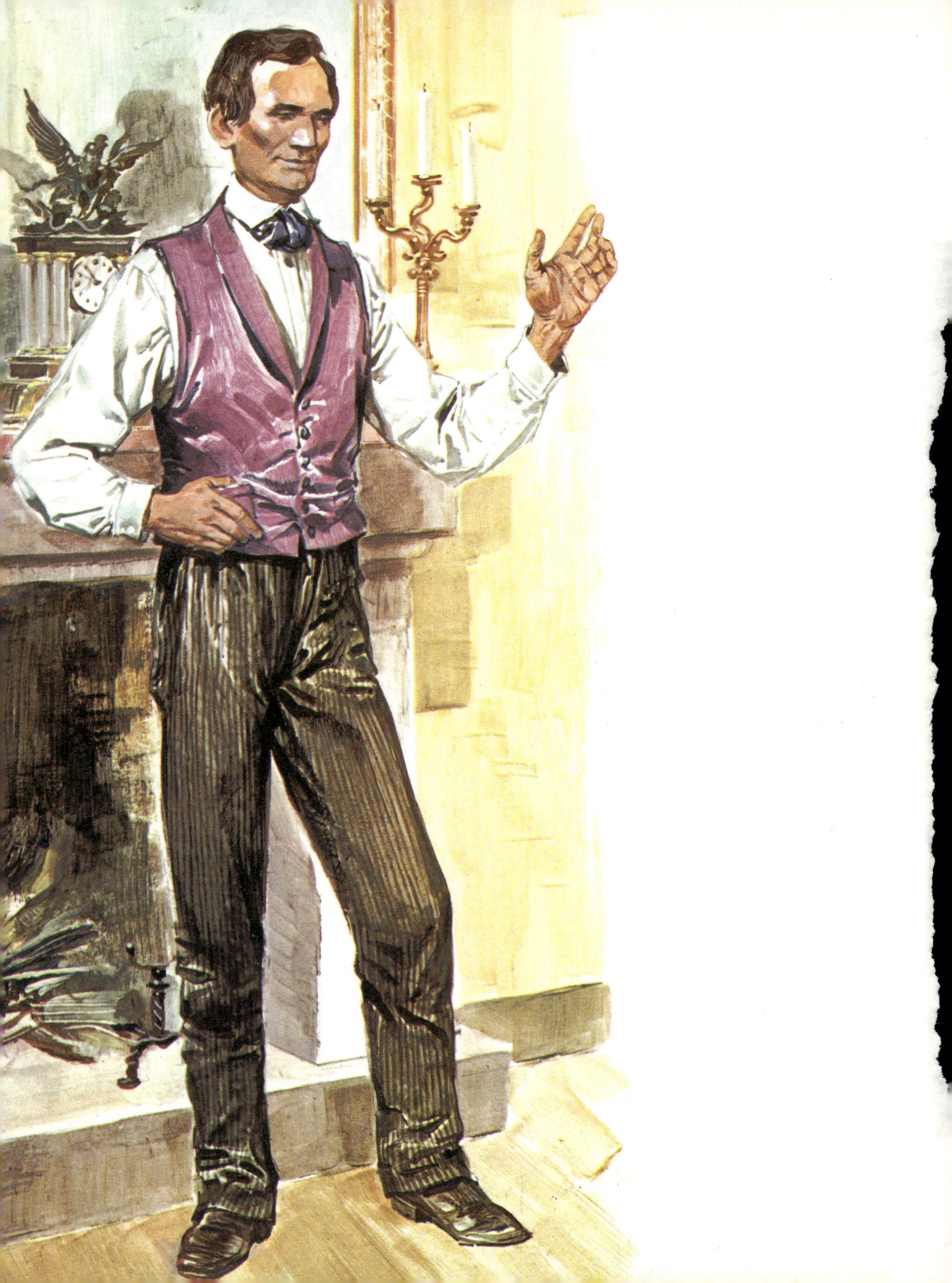

love with her. But everyone was amazed to find her taking Abe seriously.

"But Mary," her sister said, "Mr. Lincoln was raised in the backwoods."

"Even so," Mary said. "I think he'll be a big success one day."

Abe and Mary were married on November 4, 1842. He was thirty-three years old. She was twenty-three. By and by they bought a house in Springfield. They were to have four sons. Their names were Robert, Eddie, Willie, and Tad. But Eddie died of diphtheria at the age of three.

Honest Abe

In the year 1846, the people of Illinois chose Abe to represent them in the United States Congress. The Lincolns moved from Springfield to Washington, D.C.

At that time, Abe's most powerful rival was Stephen A. Douglas. In Illinois, Douglas was the leading Democratic politician. He had been elected senator. Douglas was an ambitious man. It was said that he had his eye on the White House.

Compared to Stephen Douglas, Abe seemed to be doing poorly in his career. He served one term in Congress. But then he seemed to lose interest in politics. He decided not to run again.

Abe's decision not to run again troubled Mary. She had always been interested in politics. After first meeting Abe, she was sure he would become a successful politician. She was so certain that she confided in her sister. Abe, she said, would probably be president some day.

Mary's sister thought she must be joking. "And you'll be the First Lady?" she laughed.

"Don't be surprised," Mary insisted.

Mary was still dreaming of living in the White House. Now that would never happen. She could not hide her disappointment.

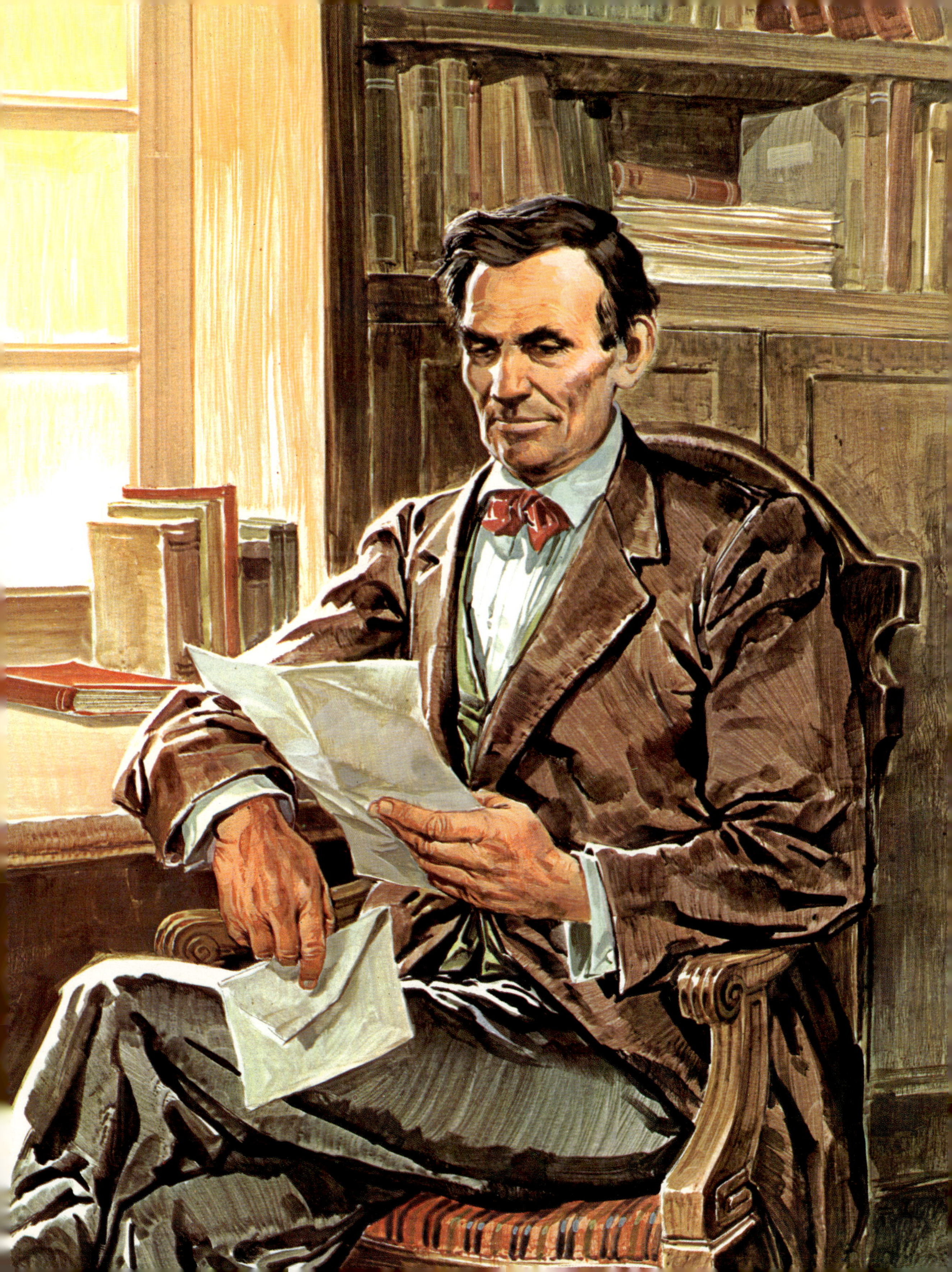

It was Abe's habit to say whatever was on his mind. He was always quick to express his views, especially about public issues. Some admired him for it. But Mary thought he could be a bit too outspoken. She thought he would make enemies. She wished very much that he would be more cautious.

Later on people would say harsh things about Mary Lincoln. Indeed, they said she was a hard person to live with. It was even claimed that the Lincolns did not get along with each other. But Abe and Mary probably got along as well as most couples.

There was a good reason why Abe did not run again for Congress. Mary may have been right. Maybe he *was* too outspoken for his own good. Back home in Illinois, some of his views were downright unpopular. Along with other Whigs, he had attacked President James Knox Polk. There had been a war against Mexico. Lincoln blamed the war on Polk, saying it was a big mistake.

To speak out against the Mexican War took courage. Many people in Illinois thought it was only right for the United States to expand its land. It was the patriotic thing to believe in at that time.

But Lincoln didn't think the war was patriotic. And he also disliked slavery. The subject was debated over and over in Congress. Whenever he could, Abe voted for laws to limit the spread of slavery.

Abe stood up for his beliefs. But sometimes this didn't help his career.

The Lincolns returned to Springfield. For the next five years Abe worked in his law office. He traveled all over the state. People liked him because he was patient. They felt they could trust him.

Once he defended the son of his friend Jack Armstrong. Jack's son Duff had been accused of murder. It was true that Duff was a weak person. And he was poor. But he had not killed anyone. To Abe, Duff was like many poor men who are unjustly suspected of doing wrong. Weren't there good *and* bad people among the poor? Honest people as well as liars?

Facing the jury, Abe thundered, "We cannot assume that because this man is poor and uneducated, hungry and desperate for money, that he is the one who committed this crime."

Duff Armstrong was judged not guilty. This case became famous, and Abe's reputation grew.

While Abe was busy with his law practice, the Whig Party was breaking up. The reason was slavery. In 1854, Senator Stephen Douglas introduced the Kansas-Nebraska Act. This act said that owning slaves in Kansas and Nebraska should be up to the white people who lived there. Most members of Congress agreed. The Kansas-Nebraska Act became the law. The new law was hated by those who were against slavery.

Northern Democrats stood together. They supported Senator Douglas. But the Whig Party had trouble agreeing. Some Whigs favored slavery. Other Whigs were opposed and wanted to keep slavery from spreading. In that same year of 1854, the Whigs who were against extending slavery split off. They joined with some Democrats who also disliked slavery. Together these two groups started a new political party. It was called the Republican Party.

Lincoln joined the Republicans. Several years later, he decided to plunge into politics again. The Republicans chose him to run for the United States Senate. His opponent was Stephen Douglas.

During the summer and fall of 1858, Lincoln and Douglas stood face to face and argued about issues. These arguments became famous as the Lincoln-Douglas debates.

Each debate was held in a different town in Illinois. The issue was slavery. Did the people of Kansas and Nebraska have the right to own slaves if they wanted to? Douglas said yes. Lincoln said Douglas was wrong. Again and again he fought hard to make himself heard. Slavery is evil, he said. It should be ended.

All over the country, newspapers printed the arguments of both candidates. Before the debates, Lincoln was only a local politician. But afterwards, he became known throughout the land.

Senator Douglas won the election. Lincoln lost, but he was to gain a greater prize. He became the leader of the Republicans. In 1860, his party chose

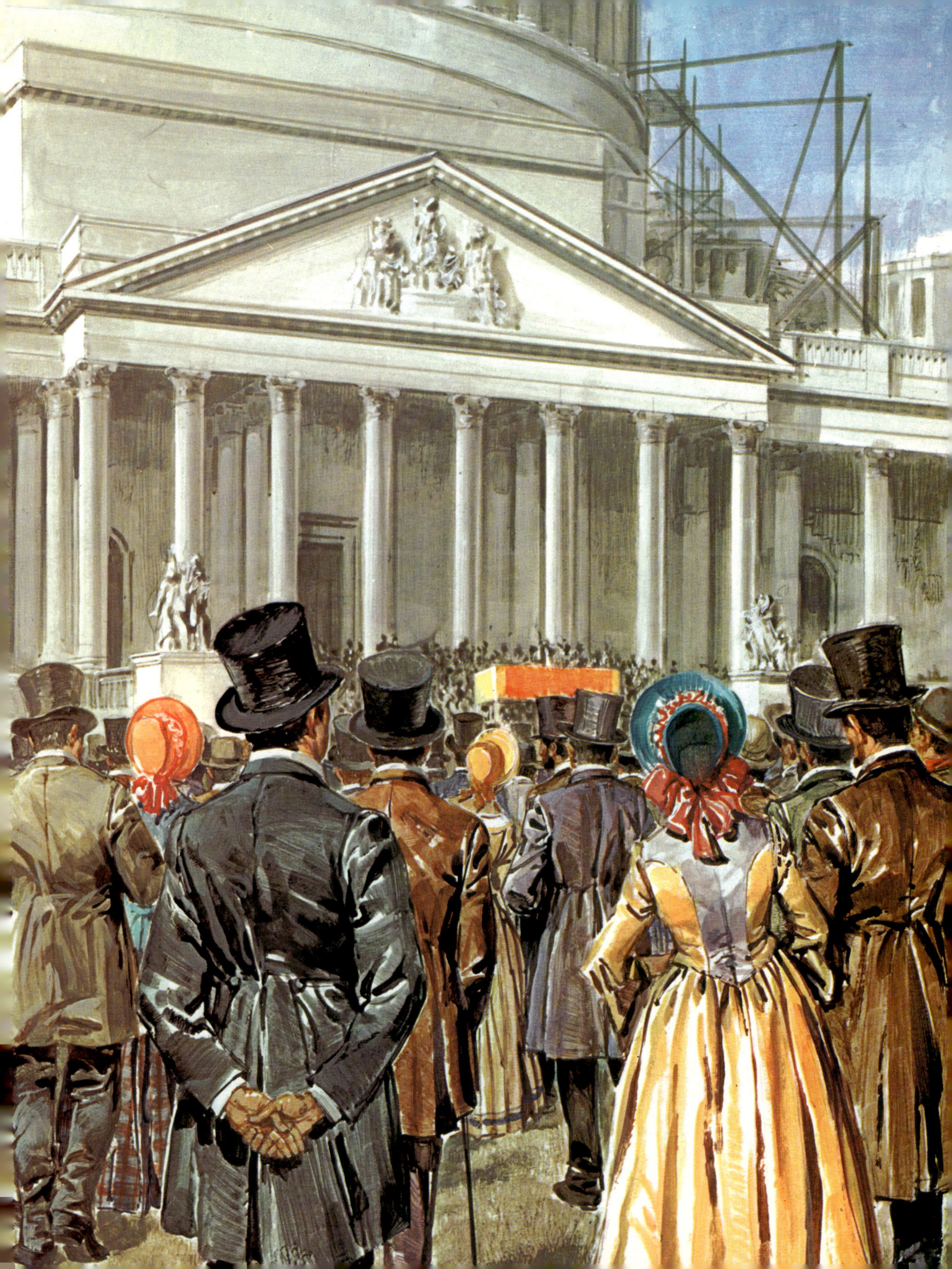

him to run for president of the United States. One of the campaign songs went like this:

Old Abe Lincoln came out of the wilderness,
  Out of the wilderness,
  Out of the wilderness,
Old Abe Lincoln came out of the wilderness
  Down in Illinois!

Abe was not old, and Illinois certainly wasn't the wilderness any more. But the tune was catchy, and he did win the election.

On March 4, 1861, Abe Lincoln took the oath of office in the nation's capital. The new President Lincoln was already facing trouble. His feelings about slavery were well known. In the South, people distrusted him. They feared he would free their slaves. Before he took office, several states angrily broke away. They decided to secede from the Union and govern themselves. Typical was South Carolina, which announced that "the union now subsisting between South Carolina and the ... United States of America is hereby dissolved."

These ominous words were echoed by six more states—Mississippi, Florida, Alabama, Georgia, Louisiana, and Texas.

Lincoln was very upset. He had done his best to prevent such a thing from happening. In his Inaugural Address, he said that he wanted to save the Union. He reminded the South that slavery would still be allowed in these states that already had slaves.

But most Southerners hated Lincoln. They did not believe what he said. Instead, they remembered a speech he had made several years earlier. In that speech he had quoted from the Bible.

"A house divided against itself cannot stand," he had warned.

And he had gone on to say, "I believe this government cannot endure permanently half slave and half free."

"I do not expect the Union to be dissolved."

"I do not expect the house to fall; but I do expect it will cease to be divided."

Many Southerners recalled the "house divided" speech. It made them feel nervous. What could they expect from such a president?

More than one American president has faced hard problems. But Lincoln's troubles may have been the worst. When he took office, some of the slave states had already left the Union. Others were threatening to go. Should he use force to bring them back into the Union?

On the other hand, what would happen if he did nothing and allowed the slave states to go? The answer was clear. The Union would be destroyed. All of his choices seemed terrible.

What was the president to do?

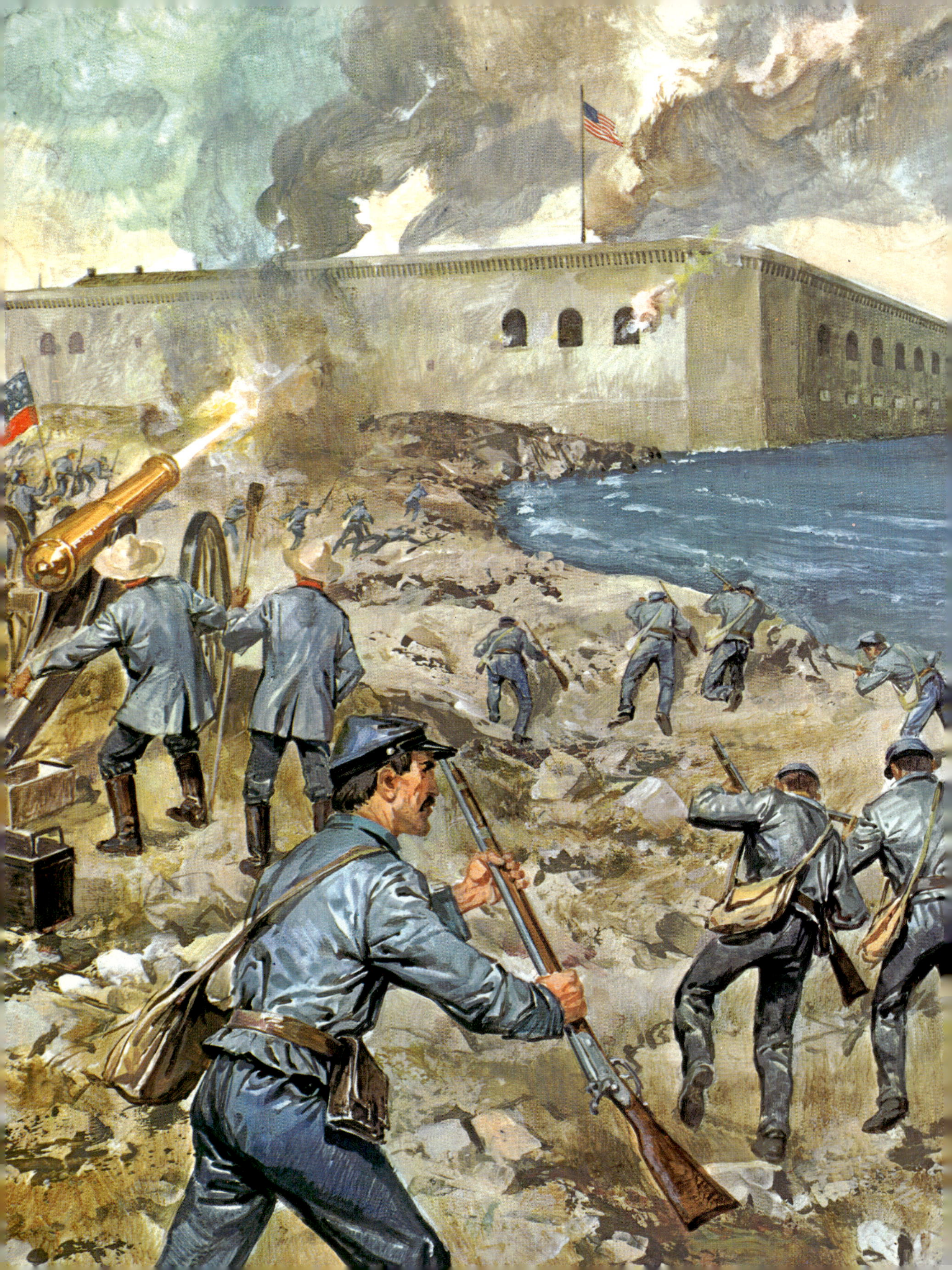

The Civil War

Out in the harbor at Charleston, South Carolina, sat Fort Sumter. This fort was the property of the United States government. However, the state of South Carolina believed that the fort was theirs. State officials asked the soldiers stationed there to surrender. But President Lincoln ordered the men to stand fast.

Southern guns blasted the fort. On April 13, 1861, it surrendered.

This event—the firing on Fort Sumter—was the spark that set off the Civil War.

A short time later, Virginia and Arkansas seceded from the Union. So did Tennessee and North Carolina. However, four slave states remained loyal. They were Delaware, Maryland, Kentucky, and Missouri. Also refusing to leave the Union was the western part of Virginia. Instead, it broke away and formed the new state of West Virginia.

The rebel states founded their own nation. They called it the Confederacy. The first capital was in Montgomery, Alabama. But later the capital was moved to Richmond, Virginia.

Jefferson Davis of Mississippi became president of the Confederacy. Its most important general was Robert E. Lee. Lee became a hero in the South. He disliked slavery. He also was against secession. But he was loyal to his home state of Virginia.

Both North and South prepared to fight. The first battle of the Civil War took place in Virginia, at a spot called Bull Run. General Irvin McDowell led the Northern army. His forces moved forward, expecting a quick victory. To their shock, the Southern army stood firm. The Southern general was Thomas Jackson. Afterwards he would be called "Stonewall" Jackson because he had refused to move. Soundly beaten, the Northern army was forced to flee.

The defeat at Bull Run was a disappointment to the president. But soon he recovered and took charge of the war.

"No sense crying over spilt milk," he said to William Seward, the secretary of state. "I've had disappointments before. I've learned never to despair."

"But what will you do now?" asked Seward.

"Try to find a general who can win this war," Lincoln told him.

He added, "And, Seward, fighting the war on the diplomatic front will be your job."

What Lincoln meant was that the Confederacy was trying to win the sympathy of England. It was Seward's job to prevent this if he could. But it would be hard. Manufacturers in England wanted the South's cotton. So it was in their interest to side with the Confederacy in the war.

Once a Union warship stopped an English ship and captured two Confederate agents who were aboard. Lincoln wanted to show the British that he meant business. Later, however, Seward told the British government he was sorry.

Meanwhile the shooting war continued. Lincoln still hoped to find a general who could win battles. He picked General John Pope. The president ordered Pope to invade Virginia. Pope got as far as Bull Run, where he met the armies of Generals Lee and Jackson. There lightning struck twice. Again, the Union forces suffered a bad defeat.

When Lincoln heard the news, he couldn't believe his ears. "Imagine," he exclaimed. "Two disasters in the same place!"

Still, President Lincoln refused to lose heart. He knew that, whatever the cost, the Union must be saved.

The Civil War caused Lincoln deep grief. When he saw the lists of dead and wounded, tears filled his eyes. He pitied their families. What right did he have to send young men to their deaths? On the other hand, what else could he do? He had to go on fighting. It was the only way to preserve the Union. He never considered the idea of giving in to the Confederacy.

In 1862, tragedy again struck the Lincoln family. Willie Lincoln, at the age of eleven, became seriously ill of typhoid and died.

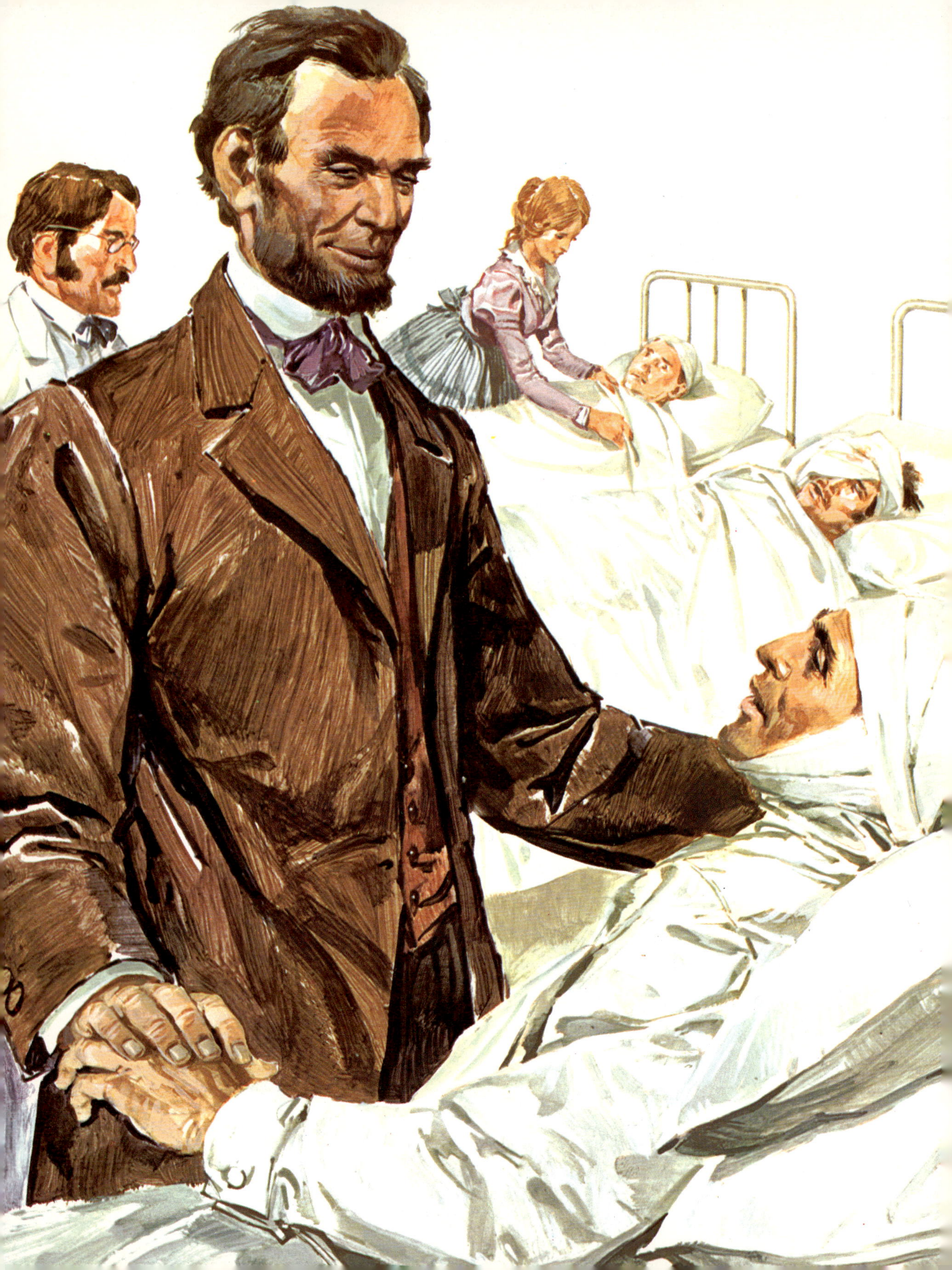

The war continued to go badly. Lincoln's thoughts seldom left the fighting. Usually his face wore a frown. Before long, the strain began to change his appearance. He looked tired and worn. Deep furrows cut his cheeks and forehead. To cover up the lines, he decided to grow a beard.

Once Lincoln told a joke. He was criticized for it. He said, "If I didn't laugh once in a while, this war would kill me."

But he found little cause for laughter. Often he traveled to hospitals near the battlefield. Visiting the wounded, he thanked them for fighting. He wanted the men to know that their great sacrifices were appreciated.

The endless war went on. By now, Lincoln was convinced that he should free the slaves. In the fall of 1862 there was a bloody battle at Antietam Creek in Maryland. Neither North nor South won.

"I would have preferred a victory," Lincoln said to the secretary of war. "But Antietam will do." Freedom for the slaves could wait no longer. He used the battle of Antietam as the occasion to issue the first draft of the Emancipation Proclamation on September 23, 1862.

In this proclamation, Lincoln declared that all slaves living in the Confederacy would become free on January 1, 1863.

As the fighting went on, there were more heartaches. None of Lincoln's generals satisfied him. He blamed General George B. McClellan for allowing Lee to escape defeat at Antietam. So he replaced McClellan with General Ambrose E. Burnside. But Lee promptly thrashed Burnside at the battle of Fredericksburg in Virginia.

Next came General Joseph Hooker. Lincoln gave him 130,000 men to attack Lee, who had half that number. The two armies met in Virginia at Chancellorsville. Caught between Lee and Stonewall Jackson, Hooker's men fled.

Until now, all the battles had been fought in the Confederacy. In the summer of 1863, General Lee decided to invade the North. He hoped for a quick victory that would end the war. The North had more factories and more supplies. If the conflict went on too long, Lee feared the South would be worn down. So he moved his army up the Shenandoah Valley. He crossed the Potomac and marched into southern Pennsylvania.

To push back the invaders, Lincoln chose General George Gordon Meade as commander. His instructions to Meade were brief.

"General Meade," he said, "I've given you all the men and guns I can. Drive General Lee out of Pennsylvania. Because if he gets any farther north, I fear we shall lose this war."

In the first days of July, the two armies met one another near the small town of Gettysburg in Pennsylvania. Among the green meadows, the battle went on for three days. On the first day, the Union forces were driven back. On the second day, there were heavy losses on both sides.

Not until the third day was the outcome of the battle finally decided. Lee's soldiers struck at the strongest part of Meade's lines. But the Union men beat them off. The following day, Lee realized he had lost. He began to retreat.

The fight at Gettysburg is one of the most famous battles in American history. It marked the turning point of the war. No longer did the North fear defeat. Likewise, the South knew they had missed their chance. The tide was turning.

The luck of the North held. Shortly after Gettysburg, another turning point in the war was reached. In Mississippi, Union forces under General Ulysses S. Grant entered Vicksburg. The Mississippi River was now open to the Union forces.

A West Point graduate, General Grant had fought bravely in the Mexican War. Then he had left the army. He tried farming and selling real estate. Once the Civil War began, Grant returned to the army. He proved to be a firm commander. Lincoln was quick to take notice of General Grant.

That fall, President Lincoln visited the battlefield at Gettysburg. On November 19, 1863, he made a speech honoring the dead. His Gettysburg Address is thought to be one of the greatest speeches of all time.

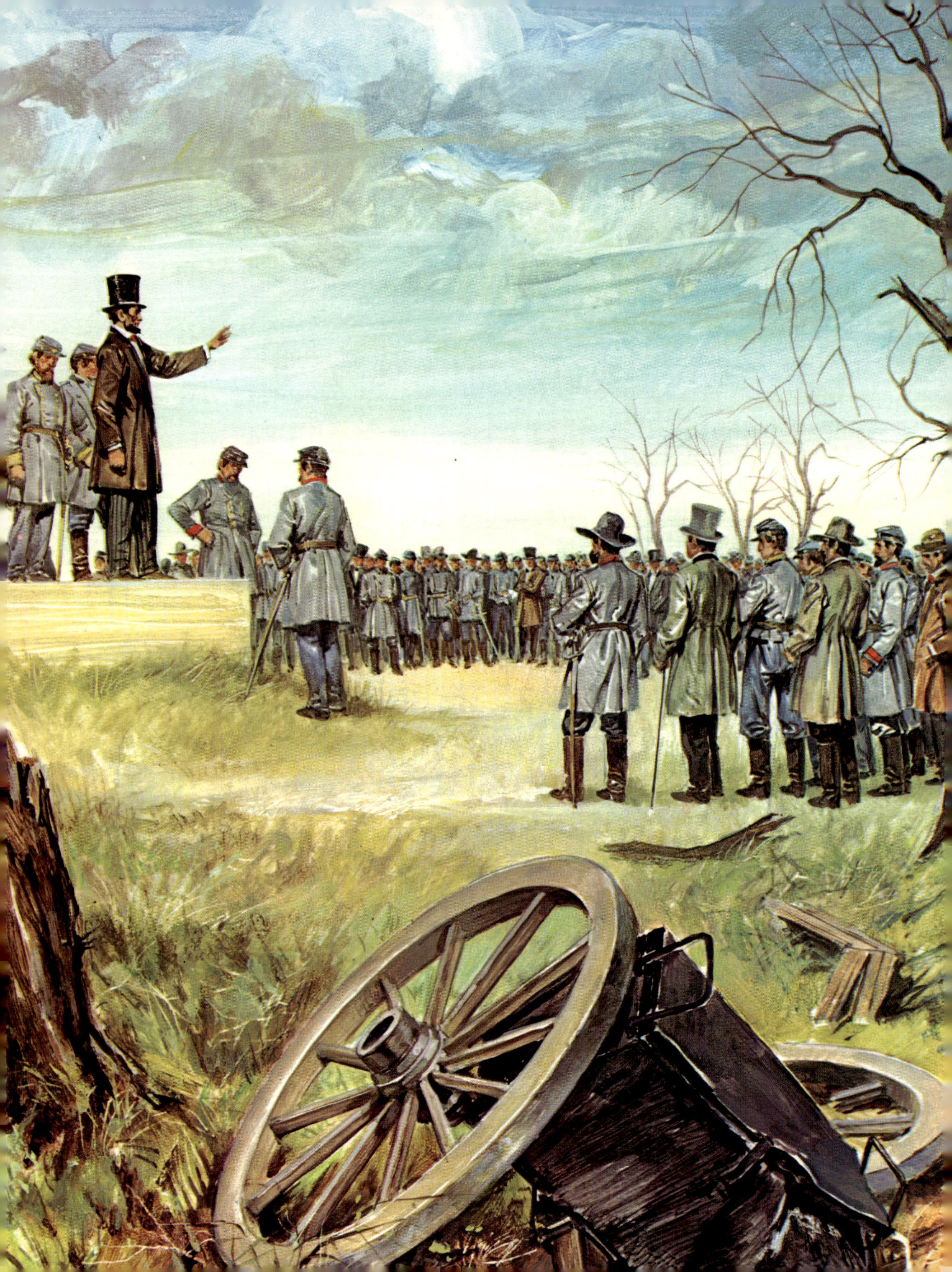

In his speech at Gettysburg, Lincoln recalled that the United States was founded on the idea of liberty and equality for everyone. He talked about the men who had died there and how they had fought to uphold those noble ideals. Finally, he made a pledge. He said that "government of the people, by the people, for the people, shall not perish from the earth."

When he finished speaking, there was hardly any clapping. The speech had lasted only two minutes. The crowd did not realize he was through.

After returning to Washington, the president felt sick. His doctors discovered that he was suffering from smallpox. In those days smallpox was a dreaded disease. And it was extremely easy to catch.

Fortunately, Lincoln's case was mild. Soon he was well enough to make jokes about his illness. Usually the White House was besieged by crowds of people seeking jobs. Suddenly they vanished, frightened away by smallpox. Lincoln joked, "But now I have something I can give to everybody."

From his bed, he followed the war. Dispatches and telegrams were eagerly read. The news was good. In Chattanooga, Tennessee, Grant won a battle. He had the Confederate Army on the run.

Lincoln continued to keep his eye on General Grant. Was this the man he had been seeking all along? Could Grant whip Robert E. Lee? Lincoln decided to take a chance. He appointed Grant to be supreme commander of the Union armies.

Brothers and Sisters, Be Free!

It was a bleak winter afternoon in Washington. At the White House, Lincoln sat at his desk. Nearby stood members of the Cabinet and other government officials.

All morning visitors had been streaming through the White House. The president had shaken many hands. Now his own hand was sore. It shook as he lifted the quill pen from the inkwell. Before him was a document to be signed. It was the final version of the Emancipation Proclamation.

For a moment Lincoln seemed to hesitate. He placed his swollen hand on the desk. Suddenly he glanced up at the others. "Never have I been more sure of doing what is right," he said. "But if my writing shows a trembling hand, people will say I had doubts about freeing the slaves."

Wanting to be sure this didn't happen, he continued to wait. Then he dipped the pen into the inkstand and wrote. His hand was steady. The date was January 1, 1863.

The Emancipation Proclamation stated that all slaves were now free in the rebelling states. It invited them to join the Union Army. To prevent bloodshed, it asked slaves not to harm their former masters.

The document ended by asking for "the considerate judgment of mankind, and the gracious favor of Almighty God."

In the South the Emancipation Proclamation caused few changes at first. Slaves were unable to take advantage of their new freedom. They still had to obey their owners.

However, change did come when the Union Army marched into the South. Slaves ran away from their masters.

They rushed to greet the invaders. Black men offered to become soldiers of the United States. Nearly two hundred thousand joined up. Black women sought protection behind the Union lines. Many carried their children. With the army they felt safe. If they lagged behind, they feared being captured and returned to slavery.

In 1864, General William Tecumseh Sherman moved into Georgia. The army of the conqueror marched from the city of Atlanta to the Atlantic Ocean. Behind them lay a trail of destruction. The Union soldiers were ordered to burn down buildings and wreck factories. Warehouses were robbed. Bridges got smashed. Railroad tracks were torn up.

General Sherman gave his men permission to do as they liked. They acted badly. From the houses of the rich they stole valuable things. They emptied barns of grain and animals. History calls this famous invasion Sherman's "March to the Sea."

All along Sherman's route, slaves fled from their owners. In a dramatic way, it showed how eager the black people were to be free. Sherman made sure they were safe from harm.

The slaves had won freedom. But Lincoln realized that freedom was only the beginning. Life would not be easy for them. Once the war ended, he could see many problems ahead. So he invited a group of black men to the White House to talk about what must be done.

"I need your help," Lincoln told them.

"But Mr. President," one of the guests said, "how can we help?"

"Peace between the races is very important," he explained. "I hope whites and blacks will be able to live as equals now. But they must get along with each other."

The former slaves agreed. With Lincoln as president, they believed it would be possible.

Today Lincoln is remembered best for freeing the slaves. He is still called "The Great Emancipator," because he signed the Emancipation Proclamation.

The Proclamation was signed in 1863. But the Civil War was not over. Indeed, the Battle of Gettysburg was still to be fought and won. And yet Lincoln felt more hopeful than he had when the war first began. His whole life he had hated slavery. Now he had kept his promise to smash it.

On that January afternoon in 1863, he left his office. He walked to the private part of the White House, where the family lived. When Mary saw him, she said, "Abraham, you look pleased."

Lincoln smiled. "I am," he said. "Mary, I wish every day could be as happy as today."

For Lincoln, the Emancipation Proclamation meant taking a wrong and making it right. But Lincoln also was a smart politician. So the document had another result. When he freed the slaves, he destroyed sympathy for the Confederacy around the world. England and France and other nations no longer wanted to do business with the South. They shifted their support to the Union.

For the rest of the war Lincoln was feeling hopeful. He smiled more often. He and Mary liked to go for drives in the country. The trees and flowers brought back memories of their life in Illinois. But the days when he was a prairie lawyer seemed very long ago.

The war went on. Under the command of General Grant, the Union Army pushed its way south into Virginia. Grant was hoping to capture the Confederate capital at Richmond. But General Lee fought back brilliantly. Grant's army suffered many losses. The number of wounded and dead kept growing. But there were available men to replace the Union dead. This was not true for Lee. He had few replacements for the soldiers he lost.

While Grant was marching toward Richmond, Lincoln was nearing the end of his first term as president. Four years had passed since he and Mary had moved into the White House. Now it was time to run for election again. His Democratic opponent in 1864 was George B. McClellan, the general.

Lincoln was elected for a second term. Nobody was more pleased than Mary Lincoln. "It certainly shows that people like you," she said.

"It shows they like my generals," he laughed. "Grant and Sherman are the ones winning the war."

It was clear that people didn't want a change until the war was over.

In his second Inaugural Address, the president looked ahead to the end of the war. The words of his speech are memorable. He spoke of completing the great cause he had undertaken—"with malice toward none; with charity for all; with firmness in the right, as God gives us to see the right...." He hoped that the nation's wounds would soon heal. Perhaps now there would be peace among all Americans.

Victory came on April 9, 1865. Robert E. Lee surrendered to General Grant at Appomattox Court

House in Virginia. After four bloody years, the Civil War was over.

It was a lovely spring. Now that the burdens of war were past, Lincoln looked forward to a quiet holiday. On Easter, he wanted to relax. Now he had time to spend with Mary and their sons.

April 14 was Good Friday. That morning the president met with his Cabinet. They talked about what he would do during his second four years in office. First he wanted to fix the state governments in the South. It was important for the South to enjoy peace and prosperity once again. Everything should be as it was before the war—but without slavery. So all morning he was busy working.

Unknown to the president, others were also busy on that very day in Washington. A group of men were plotting to kill the president. The conspirators were led by John Wilkes Booth. Booth was an actor from Virginia. Like others in the South, he was crazy with hatred. These people believed Lincoln was the person responsible for the defeat of the Confederacy.

At the White House, the afternoon passed quietly. In the evening, several friends joined Abraham and Mary. They drove to Ford's Theater to see a play called *Our American Cousin*. One of the things the Lincolns liked about Washington was attending the theater or opera. They went whenever they could. On this night, everyone was in cheerful spirits as they rode through the streets of the capital.

At Ford's Theater, they walked up a flight of stairs. The presidential box was draped with flags. They were late. The play had already begun. But the actors stopped, looked up, and bowed to the president and the First Lady. When everyone was seated, the play continued.

That year, *Our American Cousin* was very popular. Because it was a comedy, everyone in the president's box was soon laughing. Even Lincoln's bodyguards could not help paying attention to the play. Mary was pleased to see her husband's enjoyment. She reached over and took his hand.

Meanwhile, John Wilkes Booth was hanging about outside. He had a gun. He had watched as Lincoln entered the theater. He decided now was the moment to strike.

During the third act of the play, Booth hurried into Ford's. He climbed the stairs to the president's box. Those who noticed him were not suspicious. After all, he was an actor and this was a theater.

Booth quietly stepped into the box and pulled out his revolver. Before anyone could stop him he shot Lincoln in the back of the head. The president slumped forward in his chair.

To make his escape, Booth leaped from the box onto the stage. But the assassin tripped. He broke his leg. As he staggered away, people heard him shout, *"Sic Semper Tyrannis!"* This Latin phrase means "Thus Ever to Tyrants!" It is the motto of Virginia.

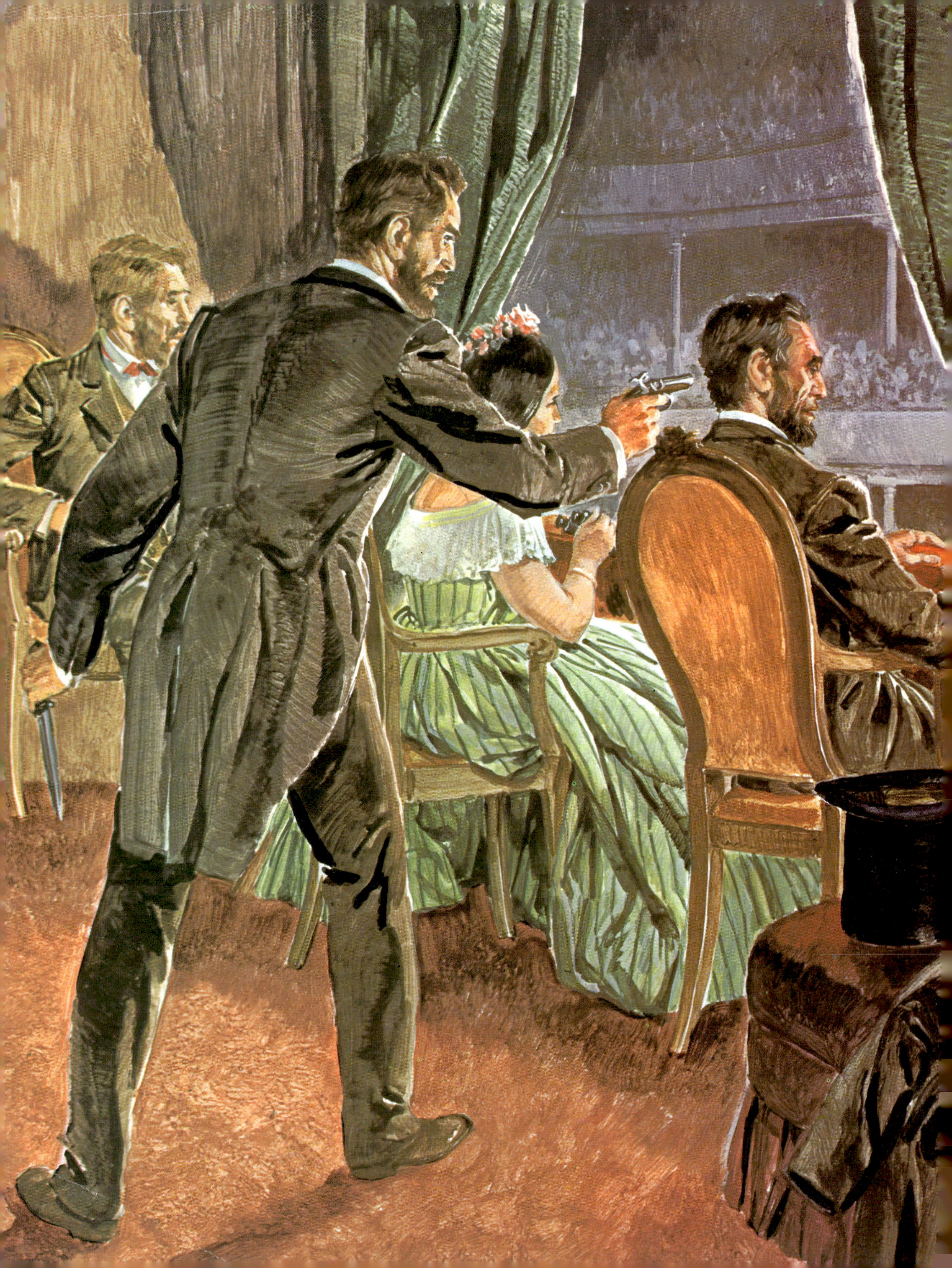

The law went after John Wilkes Booth. Soon he was captured and killed. But his mission had been successful. Lincoln was dying.

Quickly Lincoln was carried out of the theater and taken to a house across the street. Doctors fought to save his life. But he died at 7:22 A.M. the next morning. News of his murder horrified the country. It even shocked Southerners, who knew he would treat them fairly.

At the Capitol, Lincoln's body lay in state. For two days, thousands of mourners came to pay their last respects. Many people wept. They realized that they had lost a very great man.

On April 22, a train draped in black left Washington. It carried Lincoln home to Springfield, for his burial. At each station, the crowds stood silently. They watched the train move slowly by.

"Now he belongs to the ages," said Secretary of War Stanton.

No price can be placed on Abraham Lincoln's gifts to his country. He led the nation through the most terrible times—secession and civil war. He had saved the Union.

Lincoln had spoken movingly. His words are still remembered. The Gettysburg Address and the Second Inaugural Address have become part of American literature.

Abraham Lincoln is remembered all over the world as the president who freed the slaves.

The Lincoln Memorial

The Lincoln Memorial was built in Washington, D.C. to honor Abraham Lincoln, the sixteenth president of the United States. Work began on the monument on February 12, 1915, when the cornerstone was laid, and concluded when the building was dedicated in May, 1922. It was designed by Henry Bacon.

The building is made of marble and consists of a center hall which houses a huge statue of Lincoln by Daniel Chester French. On the outside of the building are 36 columns, representing the 36 states which comprised the Union when Lincoln died in 1865.

The text of Lincoln's Gettysburg Address and his Second Inaugural Address are inscribed on tablets inside the memorial.

The words of President Lincoln's Second Inaugural Address can be found inside the Lincoln Memorial. Perhaps the most famous line from that speech is, "with malice toward none; with charity for all."

Lincoln's Gettsyburg Address

The Gettysburg Address is undoubtedly Lincoln's most famous speech. He delivered it on November 19, 1863. The occasion was the dedication ceremony for the cemetery at Gettysburg, the site of the Civil War battle where 5,000 men lost their lives. The speech was printed and soon became known as a classic. Its fame spread wherever the English language was spoken at home and abroad. Countless school children have memorized the Gettysburg Address throughout the years.

Fourscore and seven years ago our fathers brought forth on this continent a new nation, conceived in liberty and dedicated to the proposition that all men are created equal.

Now we are engaged in a great civil war, testing whether that nation, or any nation so conceived and so dedicated, can long endure. We are met on a great battlefield of that war. We have come to dedicate a portion of that field, as a final resting place for those who here gave their lives that that nation might live. It is altogether fitting and proper that we should do this.

But, in a larger sense, we cannot dedicate—we cannot consecrate—we cannot hallow—this ground. The brave men, living and dead, who struggled here, have consecrated it, far above our poor power to add or detract. The world will little note nor long remember what we say here, but it can never forget what they did here. It is for us the living, rather, to be dedicated here to the unfinished work which they who fought here have thus far so nobly advanced. It is rather for us to be here dedicated to the great task remaining before us—that from these honored dead we take increased devotion to that cause for which they gave the last full measure of devotion—that we here highly resolve that these dead shall not have died in vain—that this nation, under God, shall have a new birth of freedom—and that government of the people, by the people, for the people, shall not perish from the earth.

*Abraham Lincoln
November 19, 1863*

The Emancipation Proclamation

In September of 1862, Lincoln announced to members of his Cabinet his plan to free the slaves. This plan became known as the Emancipation Proclamation, and Lincoln formally issued it on January 1, 1863. Up until this point in the war, Lincoln's main concern had not been to free the slaves, but to reunite the two halves of the country:

> *My paramount object in this struggle is to save the Union, and is not either to save or destroy slavery. If I could save the Union without freeing any slave I would do it; and if I could save it by freeing all the slaves, I would do it; and if I could do it by freeing some and leaving others alone, I would also do that.*

As president, he felt that holding the Union together was his obligation. Personally, though, he wanted to end slavery. When he was able to finally sign the Emancipation Proclamation, he felt a great sense of accomplishment, saying "I never in my life felt more certain that I was doing right than I do in signing this paper."

> *That on the 1st day of January, A.D. 1863, all persons held as slaves within any State or designated part of a State the people whereof shall then be in rebellion against the*

United States shall be then, thenceforward, and forever free; and the executive government of the United States including the military and naval authority thereof, will recognize and maintain the freedom of such persons and will do no act or acts to repress such persons, or any of them, in any efforts they may make for their actual freedom.

That the executive will on the 1st day of January aforesaid, by proclamation, designate the States and parts of States, if any, in which the people thereof, respectively, shall then be in rebellion against the United States...

...I do order and declare that all persons held as slaves within said designated States and parts of States are, and henceforward shall be free...

And I hereby enjoin upon the people so declared to be free to abstain from all violence, unless in necessary self-defense; and I recommend to them that, in all cases when allowed, they labor faithfully for reasonable wages.

...And upon this act, sincerely believed to be an act of justice, warranted by the Constitution upon military necessity, I invoke the considerate judgement of mankind and the gracious favor of Almighty God."

FROM The Emancipation Proclamation

Greeting from Garibaldi to Lincoln

The historic Emancipation Proclamation of the United States was applauded throughout the world and won the admiration of people fighting to be free everywhere.

Statements of support came from around the world. Giuseppe Garibaldi, the Italian liberator, wrote the following open letter to President Lincoln, dated August 14, 1863.

To Abraham Lincoln, Emancipator of the Slaves of the United States of America.

If, in the midst of your titanic battles, you are to lend an ear for a moment to our voices, Oh Lincoln, know that we, the free sons of Columbus send you our congratulations for the great work you have achieved.

Shaped by the thought of Christ and of Brown, you will pass into History under the name of Emancipator, a name more enviable than any royal title, than any other treasure. Because of you and the noble blood shed by Americans, an entire race has been freed from the egotistical yoke of slavery and dignity has been restored to mankind.

America, the mistress of Liberty, has opened a new age in the solemn progress of mankind. The world now wages a sad and bitter struggle for equality, and you have shown the way.

We celebrate the destruction of slavery!

We salute you, Abraham Lincoln, captain of the ship of freedom! We salute all those who have been freed and we, the free men of Italy, kiss the iron links of your chains.

The Liberals of Italy

Giuseppe Garibaldi

The Expedition of the "Thousand": the debarkation of Garibaldi at Marsala.

O CAPTAIN! MY CAPTAIN!

Abraham Lincoln inspired authors and poets, artists and sculptors. One particularly significant work is this poem by Walt Whitman written in memory of President Lincoln's assassination.

I.

O CAPTAIN! my captain! our fearful trip is done;
The ship has weathered every rack, the prize we sought is won;
The port is near, the bells I hear, the people all exulting,
While follow eyes the steady keel, the vessel grim and daring.
But O heart! heart! heart!
O the bleeding drops of red!
Where on the deck my captain lies,
Fallen cold and dead.

II.

O captain! my captain! rise up and hear the bells;
Rise up! for you the flag is flung, for you the bugle trills:
For you bouquets and ribboned wreaths, for you the shores
a-crowd-ing:
For you they call, the swaying mass, their eager faces turning,
O captain! dear father!
The arm beneath your head;
It is some dream that on the deck
You've fallen cold and dead.

III.

My captain does not answer, his lips are pale and still:
My father does not feel my arm, he has no pulse nor will.
The ship is anchored safe and sound, its voyage closed and done:
From fearful trip the victor ship comes in with object won!
Exult, O shores! and ring, O bells!
But I, with silent tread,
Walk the spot my captain lies
Fallen cold and dead.

Painting of Walt Whitman by William Smith

Manuscript of Walt Whitman's poem written in memory of Lincoln:
"O CAPTAIN! MY CAPTAIN!"

Acts on Human Rights

The Declaration of Independence, issued July 4, 1776, inspired feelings for liberty in other countries too. It stated our natural and unalienable human rights, and the obligations of governments to protect these rights. In fact, the French expressed the same sentiments and ideas in their Declaration of the Rights of Man, a prefix to their constitution of 1791.

"...We hold these truths to be self evident; that all men are created equal, that they are endowed by their creator with certain unalienable rights, that among these are life, liberty, and the pursuit of happiness. That to secure these rights governments are instituted among men, deriving their just powers from the consent of the governed; that whenever any form of government becomes destructive of these ends, it is the right of people to alter or to abolish it, and to institute new government, laying its foundation on such principles, and organizing its powers in such form, as to them shall seem most likely to effect their safety and happiness."

FROM The Declaration of Independence

In June of 1788, the Constitution of the United States went into effect. It created a federal government. The Constitution gave the United States government powers over the individual states.

> ...*The citizens of each State shall be entitled to all privileges and immunities of citizens of the several states...No person held to service or labor in the State, under the laws thereof, escaping into another, shall, in consequence of any law or regulation therein, be discharged from such service or labor, but shall be delivered up on claim of the party to whom such service or labor may be due.*
>
> FROM Article IV, Section 2
> The Constitution of the U.S.

In 1865, shortly after the end of the Civil War, the Thirteenth Amendment was added to the Constitution. It changed Article IV of the Constitution by prohibiting slavery. The government was also given the power to pass laws to enforce the amendment.

Neither slavery nor involuntary servitude, except as a punishment for crime whereof the party shall have been duly convicted, shall exist within the United States, or any place subject to their jurisdiction.

Thirteenth Amendment
The Constitution of the U.S.

The Universal Declaration of Human Rights was approved on December 10, 1948, by the General Assembly of the United Nations. Although no provisions were made by the Assembly to enforce the terms of the declaration, it has still served a purpose as a directive to the world on moral principles.

The General Assembly

Proclaims this Universal Declaration of Human Rights as a common standard of achievement for all people and all nations to the end that every individual and every organ of society, keeping this declaration constantly in mind, shall strive by teaching and education to promote respect for these rights and freedoms and by progressive measures, both national and international, to secure their universal and effective recognition and observance...

...Everyone is entitled to all the rights and freedoms set forth in this Declaration, without distinction of any kind, such as race, color, sex, language, religion, political or other opinion, national or social origin, property, birth, or other status.

...No one shall be held in slavery or servitude; slavery and the slave trade shall be prohibited in all their forms.

...Education shall be directed to the full development of the human personality and the strengthening of respect for human rights and fundamental freedoms. It shall promote understanding, tolerance, and friendship among all nations, racial or religious groups, and shall further the activities of the United Nations for the maintenance of peace.

HISTORICAL CHRONOLOGY

Life of Lincoln	Historical and Cultural Events
	1774 Philadelphia Declaration of Rights.
	1776 July 4—Declaration of Independence.
	1783 The 13 colonies become the United States.
	1789 French revolution.
	1804 Napoleon Bonaparte declares himself Emperor.

The Declaration of Independence dated July 4, 1776

The Congress of Vienna—present are the five great powers of Europe

Life of Lincoln	Historical and Cultural Events
	1805 Death of Johann Christoph Schiller, who with Goethe, was greatest German writer.
1809 Lincoln is born Hodgensville, KY, February 12.	
	1814 Napoleon abdicates.
	1815 Congress of Vienna divides Europe.
1816 Lincoln's Family moves to Indiana.	

Raftsmen Playing Cards—George Caleb Bingham

Engraving of an insurrection at Palermo, Italy, in 1820

Life of Lincoln	Historical and Cultural Events
1818 Lincoln's mother dies.	
1819-1825 Lincoln works at many jobs and studies law.	
	1820 First Italian national rebellion.
	1821 James Fenimore Cooper publishes *The Spy*.
	1823 The Monroe Doctrine issued, opposing European intervention in the Americas.

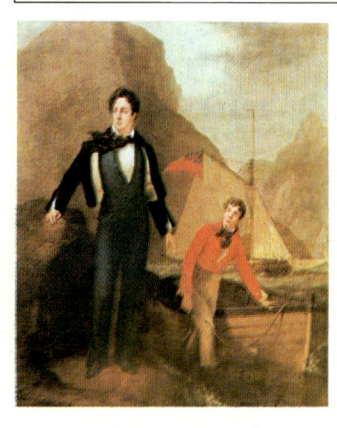

George Saunders — Painting of Lord Byron, the English writer

Simon Bolivar leads the Latin American countries in a revolt against Spain

Life of Lincoln	Historical and Cultural Events
	1824 Bryon dies in Missolonghi, Greece, of fever, while aiding rebels in the Greek fight for independence from the Turks.
	1824- Numerous Latin **1830** American countries revolt against Spain.
	1825 Erie Canal completed.
1832 Unsuccessful nomination as Whig candidate.	**1832** Goethe dies.

From the Currier and Ives Treasury: *The Rocky Mountains — Immigrants Crossing the Plains*

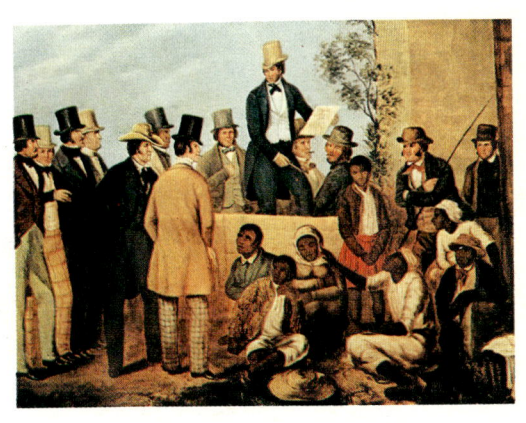

Tobacco growers at the Slave Market in Virginia — 1819

Life of Lincoln	Historical and Cultural Events
	1833 Westward expansion across the Mississippi.
1834 Lincoln elected to Illinois assembly.	
1836 Lincoln is admitted to bar.	
	1838- 1846 Mexican War.
	1840 Alessandro Manzoni writes the great nationalist Italian novel, *The Betrothed*.

Statue of Abraham Lincoln in the Lincoln Memorial—Washington, D.C.

A goldminer in his cabin—1852

Life of Lincoln	Historical and Cultural Events
1842 Leaves the assembly.	
1846 Elected to Congress.	
1849 Presents first plan for abolition of slavery/criticizes President Polk for useless war against Mexico.	**1849** California gold rush. Constitution of Frankfurt for the Unification of Germany.
	1849-1859 War of Independence for the unification of Italy.
	1850 The music of the Italian composer and patriot, Giuseppe Verdi, becomes identified with the Italian Nationalist Movement during Italy's struggle for independence from Austria.
	1851 First London Exposition for inventions, etc.

A painting of the war of independence, in Milan, for the unification of Italy

Life of Lincoln	Historical and Cultural Events
	1852 Harriet Beecher Stowe publishes *Uncle Tom's Cabin*, with its anti-slavery message.
1854- 1856 Lincoln returns to politics/joins Republican Party.	**1854- 1856** Crimean War— England, France and Piedmont fight with Turkey against Russia.
1860 Abraham Lincoln elected 16th president of the United States.	**1860** Garibaldi leads his "Thousand" into Sicily.

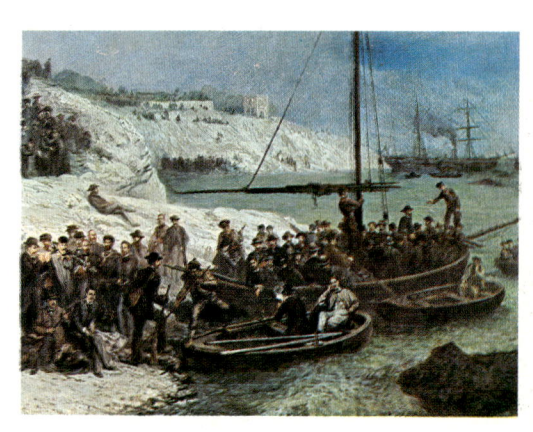

Embarkation of the Thousand, at Quarto, by T. Van Elven

A poster advertising Harriet Beecher Stowe's *Uncle Tom's Cabin*

Life of Lincoln	Historical and Cultural Events
1861 The Confederate States secede from the Union.	**1861** Kingdom of Italy proclaimed in Turin. The Czar frees the serfs in Russia.
1863 The Emancipation Proclamation, January 1. Gettysburg Address, November 19.	
1864 Lincoln reelected to the presidency.	**1864** The First Worker's International.

The Civil War: The Battle of Gettysburg—photography by Matthew Brady

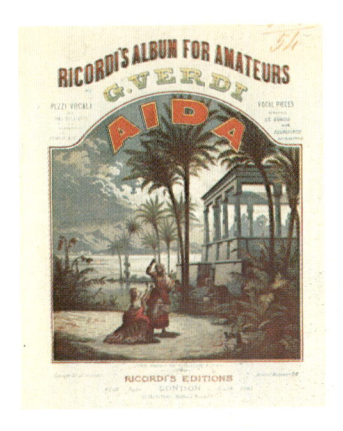

The English edition of Giuseppe Verdi's opera *Aida*

Life of Lincoln	Historical and Cultural Events
1865 South surrenders unconditionally. Lincoln enters Richmond, April 9. Lincoln assassinated, April 14.	
	1867 Defeat of French in Mexico. End of European intervention in America. Franz Joseph becomes Emperor of the Austro-Hungarian Empire.
	1870 Rome becomes capital of Italy.

Portrait of Franz Joseph, emperor of the Austro-Hungarian Empire

Picking cotton in Mississippi

INDEX

Appomatox Court House, Virginia 73, 74
Armstrong, Duff 53
Armstrong, Jack 43, 53
Assassination 74, 75, 77, 86

Bacon, Henry 78
Bar Examination 45
Bible, The 21, 57
Birth 8
Black Hawk War 43
Black Soldiers 70
Booth, John Wilkes 74, 75, 77
Burial 77
Burnside, Ambrose E. 64

Capitol 77
Civil War 41, 56, 59, 60, 61, 63, 64, 65, 67, 68, 69, 70, 71, 72, 73, 74, 77, 80, 90
Confederacy, The 56, 59, 60, 61, 63, 64, 67, 71, 72, 74
Congress, U.S. 50, 52, 53
Constitution, U.S. 83, 89, 90
Cotton 28, 35, 38, 39, 60
Crimes 28

Davis, Jefferson 59
Death 77
Declaration of Independence 88
Declaration of the Rights of Man 88
Democratic Party 44, 53, 72
Douglas, Stephen A. 50, 53, 54

Education:
  Early 9, 10, 17, 19, 21, 24
  Formal 21, 22, 24
  Legal 44, 45
Emancipation Proclamation 63, 68, 69, 71, 82, 83, 84
England 38, 60, 61, 72

Ferryman 8, 24, 26, 28
Fighting 43
Ford's Theater 74, 75
Fort Sumter 59
France 72
French, Daniel Chester 78

Garibaldi, Giuseppe 84, 85
Gentry, Allen 26, 27, 28
Gentry, James 26, 27, 28
Gettysburg Address 65, 71, 77, 78, 80, 81
Gettysburg, Pennsylvania 64, 65, 80
Grant, Ulysses S. 65, 67, 72, 73
"Great Emancipator" 71

Hanks, Dennis 12, 16, 19, 30
Hanks, John 30, 31, 33, 34, 35, 38, 39
Historical Chronology 92, 93, 94, 95, 96, 97, 98, 99, 100, 101
"Honest Abe" 44
Hooker, Joseph 64
Human Rights 88, 89, 90, 91
Hunting 9, 10, 12, 13

Illinois 30, 43, 44, 47, 50, 52, 54, 56, 72
Illinois House of Representatives 44
Inaugural Addresses 56, 73, 77, 78, 79
Indians 15, 16, 30, 43

Jackson, Andrew 39, 44
Jackson, Thomas "Stonewall" 60, 61, 64
Jobs 24, 26, 31, 43, 44, 53
Johnston, Elizabeth 20
Johnston, John 20, 31, 33
Johnston, Matilda 20
Johnston, Sarah Bush 20

Kansas-Nebraska Act 53

Lee, Robert E.   59, 61, 64, 65, 67, 72, 73
Legal Career   30, 44, 45, 53
Legree, Simon   41
Lincoln, Abraham (Sr.)   10, 13, 15
Lincoln-Douglas Debates   54
Lincoln, Eddie   49
Lincoln, Joshua   13, 15
Lincoln, Mary Todd   47, 49, 50, 52, 71, 72, 74, 75
Lincoln Memorial   78, 79
Lincoln, Mordecai   13, 15, 16
Lincoln, Nancy Hanks   7, 8, 9, 12, 16, 17
Lincoln, Robert   49
Lincoln, Sarah   8, 13, 15, 17, 19, 20
Lincoln, Sarah Bush Johnston   20, 21
Lincoln, Tad   49
Lincoln, Thomas   7, 8, 9, 10, 12, 13, 15, 16, 17, 20, 30
Lincoln, Willie   49, 61
Log Cabin   8, 9, 10, 31

"March to the Sea"   70
Marriage   45, 49
McClellan, George B.   64, 72
McDowell, Irvin   60
Meade, George Gordon   64, 65
Mexican War   52, 65
Milk Sickness   16

North, The   38, 41, 43, 60, 63, 64

O CAPTAIN! MY CAPTAIN   86, 87
Offut, Denton   31, 33, 39
Our American Cousin   74, 75

Political Career   39, 43, 44, 47, 50, 54, 56
Polk, James Knox   52
Pope, John   61
"Prairie Lawyer"   45
Presidency   56, 72

"Rail-Splitter," The   31
Reading   21, 24, 44
Republican Party   54
Rutledge, Ann   45

Secession   56, 59, 60, 77
Senate, U.S.   54
Seward, William H.   60
Sherman, William Tecumseh   70, 72
Slavery   34, 35, 36, 37, 38, 39, 41, 52, 53, 54, 56, 57, 59, 63, 68, 69, 70, 71, 74, 82, 83, 84, 85, 90, 91
Smallpox   67
Smith, William   87
South, The   35, 39, 41, 56, 57, 59, 60, 63, 64, 69, 72, 74
Sparrow, Betsy   12, 16
Sparrow, Tom   12, 16
Stanton, Edwin M.   77
Steamboats   24, 26, 28
Stowe, Harriet Beecher   41
Supreme Court, The   44
Surrender   73

Thirteenth Amendment   90
Tobacco   28
Typhoid   61

Uncle Tom   41
Uncle Tom's Cabin   41
Union, The   56, 57, 59, 61, 65, 67, 68, 69, 70, 77, 82
United Nations   90, 91
Universal Declaration of Human Rights   90, 91

Washington, D.C.   47, 50, 68, 78
Washington, George   24
West Point Military Academy   65
Whig Party   44, 52, 53, 54
Whitman, Walt   86, 87
White House, The   39, 41, 50, 67, 68, 71, 72, 74

BOOKS FOR FURTHER READING

Abe Lincoln Grows Up by Carl Sandburg, Harcourt Brace Jovanovich, 1985.

Abe Lincoln: Log Cabin to the White House by Sterling North, Random House, 1963.

Abraham Lincoln by Ingri and Parin D'Aulaire, Doubleday, 1987.

Abraham Lincoln by Katie B. Smith, Julian Messner, 1987.

Abraham Lincoln: The Great Emancipator by Augusta Stevenson, Macmillan, 1986.

If You Grew Up with Abraham Lincoln by Ann McGovern, Scholastic, 1985.

Lincoln: A Photobiography by Russell Freedman, Clarion, 1987.

Mr. Lincoln's Inaugural Journey by Mary K. Phelan, Crowell Jr., 1972.

True Stories About Abraham Lincoln by Ruth B. Gross, Scholastic, 1988.